"Rick Hess continues to expose . . . . of transforming public schooling in America. An esteemed scholar who is always willing to speak his mind and shake up the status quo through innovation, he is someone we should listen to as we apply policy to practice. I look forward to hearing the dialogue that this book will create."

—Michelle M. Rhee, Chancellor, District of Columbia Public Schools

"In *Education Unbound* Rick Hess argues persuasively that system rigidity is preventing school success at scale. Hess believes we must promote flexibility so that schools can find their own way to recruit talented teachers, focus on results, and reward success. Once again, Hess has offered a fresh perspective by challenging us to question the status quo in public education."

—Kathleen McCartney, Dean and Gerald S. Lesser Professor in Early Childhood Development Harvard Graduate School of Education

"Rick Hess's book *Education Unbound* offers a refreshing approach to our education dilemma. It is well past time we face the reality that the "find and fix" methods we have so energetically and honestly applied to our educational problems has not worked and continuing the same is unwise. This book is a must-read for those who seek authentic educational improvement."

—Rod Paige, U.S. Secretary of Education, 2000–2005

"In *Education Unbound,* Frederick Hess continues his call to entrepreneurship as an essential force in improving education in the United States. Hess approaches reform with an economist's sense of efficiency and an educator's passion for effective teaching and student learning. In this volume, Hess argues that instead of lubricating current antiquated education systems we should cultivate new "greenfield" landscapes. His arguments and examples will give hope to many educators who refuse to be resigned to dysfunction and are ready to overturn the status quo."

—Anthony S. Bryk, President, The Carnegie Foundation for the Advancement of Teaching

"As the President and Secretary of Education urge the country to "Race to the Top," Rick Hess cautions that lasting school reform requires us to first attend to the fundamental structural obstacles that will keep us from success. Hess demonstrates that we will need equal doses of humility and courage if we are to make the most of this unique opportunity. Every state policymaker, educator, and entrepreneur committed to leveraging this moment for transformational change should start by grounding themselves in Hess's trenchant analysis of what mistakes we've already made and how we can avoid making them again."

—Mike Johnston, Colorado State Senator, District 33

"Provocative and important. Hess puts on paper the ideas and ethos that are defining leading-edge education reform efforts today. Essential reading for educators, policymakers, and everyone who understands why it's essential that we transform our education system."

—Andrew J. Rotherham, Co-founder and Publisher of
Education Sector and author of Eduwonk.com

EDUCATION
UNBOUND

ASCD MEMBER BOOK

Many ASCD members received this book as a
member benefit upon its initial release.

Learn more at: **www.ascd.org/memberbooks**

SUSTAINABLE
FORESTRY
INITIATIVE

Certified Fiber Sourcing
www.sfiprogram.org

ASCD cares about Planet Earth.
This book has been printed on environmentally friendly paper.

EDUCATION
UNBOUND

THE PROMISE AND PRACTICE OF
GREENFIELD SCHOOLING

FREDERICK M. HESS

Alexandria, Virginia

1703 N. Beauregard St. • Alexandria, VA 22311-1714 USA
Phone: 800-933-2723 or 703-578-9600 • Fax: 703-575-5400
Web site: www.ascd.org • E-mail: member@ascd.org
Author guidelines: www.ascd.org/write

Gene R. Carter, *Executive Director;* Nancy Modrak, *Publisher;* Scott Willis, *Director, Book Acquisitions & Development;* Julie Houtz, *Director, Book Editing & Production;* Katie Martin, *Editor;* Sima Nasr, *Senior Graphic Designer;* Mike Kalyan, *Production Manager;* Barton Matheson Willse & Worthington, *Typesetter;* Carmen Yuhas, *Production Specialist*

Printed in the United States of America. Cover art © 2010 by ASCD. ASCD publications present a variety of viewpoints. The views expressed or implied in this book should not be interpreted as official positions of the Association.

All Web links in this book are correct as of the publication date below but may have become inactive or otherwise modified since that time. If you notice a deactivated or changed link, please e-mail books@ascd.org with the words "Link Update" in the subject line. In your message, please specify the Web link, the book title, and the page number on which the link appears.

ASCD Member Book, No. FY10-5 (Feb. 2010, P). ASCD Member Books mail to Premium (P), Select (S), and Institutional Plus (I+) members on this schedule: Jan., PSI+; Feb., P; Apr., PSI+; May, P; July, PSI+; Aug., P; Sept., PSI+; Nov., PSI+; Dec., P. Select membership was formerly known as Comprehensive membership.

PAPERBACK ISBN: 978-1-4166-0913-1   ASCD product #109040
Also available as an e-book (see Books in Print for the ISBNs).

Quantity discounts for the paperback edition only: 10–49 copies, 10%; 50+ copies, 15%; for 1,000 or more copies, call 800-933-2723, ext. 5634, or 703-575-5634. For desk copies: member@ascd.org.

Library of Congress Cataloging-in-Publication Data

Hess, Frederick M.
    Education unbound : the promise and practice of greenfield schooling / Frederick M. Hess.
        p. cm.
    Includes bibliographical references and index.
    ISBN 978-1-4166-0913-1 (pbk. : alk. paper)
    1. Educational change—United States.   2. Educational innovations—United States.   I. Title.

    LA217.2.H48 2010
    370.973—dc22

                                                                    2009041959

20 19 18 17 16 15 14 13 12 11 10   1 2 3 4 5 6 7 8 9 10 11 12

EDUCATION
UNBOUND

ACKNOWLEDGMENTS

I WOULD LIKE TO thank a number of individuals for their invaluable advice and support in making this volume possible.

I owe a special thanks to Loren Baron, Thomas Gift, Morgan Goatley, Monica Higgins, Rosemary Kendrick, Ted Kolderie, Doug Lynch, Bruno Manno, Michele McLaughlin, Tom Vander Ark, and Steven Wilson for their gracious willingness to peruse the manuscript and provide valuable feedback. And I'd like to thank Eric Adler, Norman Atkins, Chris Barbic, Matt Candler, Celine Coggins, Ben Cope, Tim Daly, Colleen Dippel, Heather Driscoll, Mike Feinberg, David Harris, Ryan Hill, Joel Horwich, Jason Kamras, Sheryl Linsky, Steve Mancini, Michelle Rhee, Larry Rosenstock, David Saba, Eric Schwarz, Deanna Sheaffer, David Steiner, Dacia Toll, Mark Vineis, Rajiv Vinnakota, Charles Zogby, and all the others who contributed insights or experiences to this effort.

I'd particularly like to offer my heartfelt thanks to the multitalented and generally terrific Juliet Squire for her crucial role in researching, editing, and crafting this book. As ever, I owe the deepest appreciation to the American Enterprise Institute and its president, Arthur Brooks, for the remarkable support and backing that allow me to pursue this work. And I owe a special thanks to my editor, Scott Willis, for his patience, support, and guidance.

As always, I'd like to thank Joleen for all her love and understanding, through this project as through so many others.

Finally, it goes without saying that any mistakes, flaws, or inanities are entirely mine and mine alone.

PREFACE

THE GENESIS OF THIS volume traces not to my years as an academic and researcher but to my time as an educator: teaching in East Baton Rouge Parish, Louisiana, and mentoring student teachers in Boston. In those days, I constantly wondered how so many well-intentioned people could have collectively created such a frustrating morass and why school systems seemed to revel in Kafkaesque routines.

When I first applied for teaching jobs in January 1990, I eagerly sent more than 100 letters of inquiry to a variety of districts . . . and got zero responses. (I didn't realize that school districts weren't geared to respond to inquiries sent before the spring.) Eventually, I was hired in Baton Rouge, in part to start an Advanced Placement Economics course, which would have been Louisiana's third. But I was first reassigned to a middle school, and then shifted back to a high school just days before classes began. It was there that I watched a succession of hurdles—textbook acquisition, classroom assignments, and my permissible course load—put the kibosh on my planned AP Economics class. I knew I was not going to make it as a classroom instructor when my offer to teach the course during my "free period" got me into hot water with the administration.

The data suggest that plenty of today's teachers feel the same kind of frustration I felt. The U.S. Department of Education's Schools Staffing Survey reports that 9 in 10 of the nation's teachers somewhat or strongly agree that routine duties and paperwork interfere with their teaching.[1] The generally cheery 2008 MetLife Survey of the American Teacher finds that half of teachers report spending 25 percent or more of their time on discipline and administrative work.[2]

The problem is that the dysfunction that limns our school systems is like the air we breathe: it's so familiar and accepted that, after a while, we take it for granted. We forget that things might be otherwise—that there's no reason choosing to be an educator should mean accepting bureaucracy, standardization, and inept management. Perhaps it takes an outside perspective to recognize how destructive the status quo really is. One business school management professor I spoke with, whose students include aspiring school leaders, had this to say:

> [My students] shared stories about bureaucratic rules focused on a range of topics: from dealing with problem people to rules about how many pictures you can have on your desk, about how to decorate your office, and about closing the window blinds when you leave at the end of the day. . . . The former I expected, but the latter types of rules I didn't. These, I think, are symptomatic of deep, pathological problems.

This is a book for all educators who have gnashed their teeth in frustration while battling to get textbooks from the central office and asked, "Does it have to be this way?" This is a book for every principal who has wrestled with bureaucracy to procure a new reading program or retain a great teacher and wondered, "Does this have to be so hard?" This is a book for every superintendent who has watched the human resources department come up short on key staffing needs and wondered, "Can't we do better?" This is a book for curriculum designers and philanthropists who have seen promising ideas succeed in pilot programs but decay over time and wondered, "Isn't there some way to make this stick?" This is a book for all who wonder what it would take to forge a world in which educators can truly focus on the work of teaching and learning.

In putting pen to paper, I've written with three distinct audiences in mind:

• The community of practitioners and educational leaders frustrated with the status quo and seeking to launch new schools, attract and cultivate talent, and get their hands on better services and instructional tools;

• Policymakers, advocates, funders, and civic and business leaders tired of the disheartening results of faddish reforms and eager for more effective problem solving; and

• Academics, undergraduates, graduate students, and aspiring educators hungry for a more promising approach to educational challenges.

This volume is not a how-to guide for entrepreneurs. It is an introduction to a way of thinking about improving teaching and learning that is profoundly different from the approaches usually encountered in schools and universities or among policymakers. I will argue that although greenfield schooling is, as yet, unfamiliar to many, it offers the most promising course for 21st century school improvement. In the pages ahead, readers will encounter candid comments from an array of reformers, funders, and entrepreneurs who have graciously offered their experiences to inform this volume. All quotes, unless otherwise attributed, are drawn from personal communications.

Before we proceed, I want to say a few words about how I anticipate some readers may react to the focus and tone of the discussion. Plainly speaking, greenfield schooling is dominated by organizations that more than a few educators, parents, and public officials view with suspicion. Moreover, any discussion of "entrepreneurial" schooling raises hackles, especially as it unapologetically focuses on issues of cost-effectiveness and productivity. My hope is that readers will keep two points in mind. First, these organizations are attempting to address stubborn problems—such as school staffing and urban achievement—in order to benefit children. For good and ill, staff at ventures like the KIPP (Knowledge Is Power Program) Academies and Achievement First are a modern parallel to the optimistic and idealistic Peace Corps volunteers of the 1960s. Whatever their faults, they are as passionate about serving kids as the best classroom educators are. With regard to the for-profits, like K12 Inc. and EdisonLearning, I'd note that most financial types think schooling is a lousy place for a profit-hungry entrepreneur, I've found their employees care just as much about kids as district employees do, and I'm personally OK with someone making a buck off of education so long as the kids benefit from the deal.

Educators' common aim is to serve students better and to promote teaching and learning. Although there is a tendency in schooling to shrink from the language of cost-effectiveness or productivity, these words mean only that dollars, time, and energy devoted to teaching and learning should make the greatest possible contribution to teaching and learning. Whether we like the terminology or not, we can all embrace the intuitive sense behind it. If district hiring is more costly than it needs to be, or if the district is buying an assessment system that is less useful to teachers than an alternative, the end result is that students will be worse served. Aggressively squeezing out inefficiency is not pro- or anti-schooling; it is simply responsible stewardship of both students and schools.

Finally, those who insist that only the conventional schoolhouse can foster an authentic student-teacher relationship and that talk of Web-based or non-traditional provision is a worrisome trend should at least consider the take of Dianna Miller, an Advanced Placement Economics teacher for Florida Virtual School, who says, "My [online] students tell me that I know more about them than any of their classroom teachers, but I've never even seen them."[3] The reality of an increasingly wired world makes it imperative that we continually revisit assumptions about what constitutes good teaching and valuable learning.

This is a book for educators, educational leaders, public officials, funders, civic leaders, researchers, would-be reformers, and all those others who know how incredibly hard it is to drive lasting improvement and wonder whether there might be a better way. Most books on education explain why a particular instructional technique or curricular approach will help. This volume considers what to do if the fundamental problem is not *this practice* or *that approach* but a *system* that prevents good practices from ever being pursued on more than a scattershot basis. And the answer begins with creating greenfield—not merely the opportunity to solve problems but the ability to do so in a hospitable, quality-conscious, and dynamic environment that puts more emphasis on the needs of kids than on our comfortable routines.

The key to breakthrough improvement is not engineering intricate new solutions but tilling the field to improve the possibility that dramatic and sustainable improvements will take root. Doing so entails rethinking norms, institutions, and routines so that educators and a new generation of problem solvers can address age-old challenges of teaching and learning more effectively in the 21st century. This book sketches a vision of how that can be done. Shall we begin?

I

WHAT IS GREENFIELD SCHOOLING?

GREENFIELD **IS A TERM OF ART** typically used by investors, engineers, or builders to refer to an area where there are unobstructed, wide-open opportunities to invent or build. It is not a term one hears much in K–12 education. This is no surprise. For all their virtues, schools in the United States are not noted for their embrace of creative problem solvers. Indeed, most educators labor in bureaucratic, rule-driven school systems that owe more credit to the practices of early 20th century factory management than to any notion of how to foster great teaching and learning in the 21st century.

It may be easiest to understand greenfield as a venue that provides rich opportunities for new ventures. In real estate, *greenfield* refers to a piece of previously undeveloped land, one that is in its natural state or used for agriculture. In the jargon of software engineering, a *greenfield project* is a new application that operates without any constraints imposed by prior versions. A *greenfield labor agreement* is the first deal struck between a company and its employees.

In schooling, creating greenfield requires scrubbing away our assumptions about districts, schoolhouses, teacher training, and other familiar arrangements so that we might use resources, talent, and technology to support teaching and learning in smarter, better ways. For example, while locally governed school districts made sense in an earlier era, advances in transportation and communication mean it is no longer obvious that managing 20 schools with varying missions in one community is easier than managing a network of more similar schools across several communities. The ability to deliver instruction across

1

thousands of miles means that students may receive more individualized, interactive, and rigorous instruction from tutors halfway around the world than they can in a local classroom. Open source technology means that districts need not spend billions procuring textbooks that will rapidly become outdated.

Schools and districts struggle to adapt to the larger changes taking place, but this may be an ill-fated pursuit. The pressures of existing rules, routines, contracts, and culture can make it difficult for new practices to stick. Our familiar schools and districts may be, by design, ill-suited to seize upon these changes, just as established newspapers were when it came to the new tools and opportunities presented by online publishing.

Today, dynamic educators push through frustrations, do end runs around bureaucracies, and operate with a wink and a nod to get the staff they require or the resources they need. Far too many educators can relate to stories like that of Larry Rosenstock, who worked in the Cambridge, Massachusetts, schools for 11 years before being driven—by sheer frustration—to launch what would become the acclaimed High Tech High charter school in San Diego. Rosenstock's tales from Cambridge often sound like fodder for an episode of *The Office*. He recalls battling to update his school's scheduling software, which was "pre-Copernican" in its class rotation. "We had MIT kids who wanted to volunteer in science classes," he says, "but under that schedule, if they came every Tuesday afternoon, they'd only be working with the same kids every seventh week." Rosenstock and his crew tried to change the schedule, but in a meeting of teachers, one said, "We can't change the schedule, the schedule won't let us." Rosenstock sighs. "It's a 353-year-old public high school, and every time somebody did something stupid, [the administration] added new rules. They don't take away rules, they just add new rules, so it gets to a point where there's no oxygen left."

When Rosenstock left Cambridge to found High Tech High in 2000, he knew that building a new school would require addressing real estate financing, authorization, fundraising, regulations, and dozens of other stepping stones. Still, Rosenstock says, "I spent 20 years doing turnaround artistry, and I spent the past decade doing new school creation. There might be some complications and risks to new school creation, but as complicated and challenging as it may be, it is way easier than trying to turn around a pre-existing school." In fact, he argues, "Because pre-existing schools are ossified by culture, employment agreements, expectations, and so on, building on greenfield is actually far easier."

Today, educators who are eager to pioneer new strategies or take advantage of new technologies find themselves stymied by contracts, wrangling with cautious administrators, and forced to negotiate rafts of rules, stacks of paperwork, and resistance from skeptical veterans. Young educators learn early on that keeping their heads down is often the safest path to professional advancement, and that closing their classroom doors is the simplest way to shut out the constant swelter of new reforms. The best educators have come to accept the struggle with bureaucracy as their due and to compensate for ineffective colleagues. Greenfield schooling seeks to create a world more welcoming to Larry Rosenstock and his kin. It seeks school systems open to reinvention and dynamic problem solving, and a sector welcoming to promising new ventures that extends the same opportunities to talented, hard-working professionals in education that enliven professional lives and fuel success in other realms.

Greenfield schooling presumes that the greatest challenge for improving teaching and learning is the creaky, rule-bound system in which they unfold. While we routinely point to a need for new instructional, curricular, and pedagogical strategies or debate the mixed results of those in place, greenfielders deem school systems so hobbled that even sensible efforts will fall short. They worry that today's regulations, organizations, and routines make it nearly impossible to implement any of these innovative strategies with fidelity, at scale, for a sustained period. This means that the key problems facing K–12 education are ultimately systemic, rather than instructional, and that great teaching and curricula will only work if we first address these larger burdens. This is precisely the greenfield reform strategy: Create an environment that invites new solutions to surface and provides the infrastructure necessary for such ventures to succeed.

Greenfield can be created inside or outside traditional districts. Dynamic public school leaders in districts like Chicago, New York, and Washington, DC, have created opportunities and scaffolding that promote entrepreneurial successes. For example, when Joel Klein became chancellor of the New York City Department of Education, he declared his intention to make the system the "Silicon Valley of the charter school movement," recruiting the nation's best charter schools to New York, making it easier for charters to obtain buildings, and providing charters with funding levels more on par with traditional district schools.[1] Dacia Toll, president of Achievement First, a network of more than a dozen college-prep charter schools for urban students, notes, "Providing facilities on equal terms and letting dollars largely follow the child has allowed Achievement First to be bigger after four years in New York than after 10 in Connecticut." The new landscape has prompted Achievement First to largely abandon its original growth plans in Connecticut and to concentrate instead on opening its heralded schools in New York.

What Exactly *Is* Entrepreneurship?

Entrepreneurship is a slippery notion. In the United States, it is often a catchall label for launching a business. A more useful definition is offered by economist Joseph Schumpeter, who explained that entrepreneurship serves to introduce new goods and services, tools, or strategies. He argued that human progress is primarily driven not by the gradual improvement of familiar organizations but by new ventures displacing yesterday's titans in a vigorous, dynamic cycle of "creative destruction."[2]

Peter Drucker famously described entrepreneurship as a process of purposeful innovation intended to improve productivity, efficiency, or quality. In other words, entrepreneurship is not simply about *change*; it is about using untapped tools, knowledge, talent pools, or management approaches to solve problems more effectively. Today, the entrepreneurial presumption is that the path to improvement is necessarily messy. Management scholars have estimated that 60 percent of all new product development efforts are abandoned before the product ever reaches the market, and nearly half of the products that do make it to market ultimately fail.[3]

Entrepreneurship is *not* about blindly celebrating innovation or every nifty-sounding idea. If anything, we have had too much educational innovation over the years. A decade ago, in a book titled *Spinning Wheels*, I reported that the typical urban school district had launched at least 13 major reforms in a three-year span during the 1990s[4]—a new reform every three months! That is like trying to build on quicksand. It means that nothing has time to work, employees get worn out, and systems are left fragmented and dotted with orphaned programs.

Today, an array of charter school ventures like the KIPP Academies, YES Prep, Aspire Public Charter Schools, and Achievement First are addressing stubborn challenges by pursuing familiar notions of good teaching and effective schooling in impressively coherent, disciplined, and strategic ways. Other ventures, such as Citizen Schools, EdisonLearning, The New Teacher Project, K12 Inc., Wireless Generation, and New Leaders for New Schools, have devised dramatically new approaches to tackle important challenges. (Don't worry if these names are unfamiliar; you'll learn more about them in the pages ahead.)

Even these marquee entrepreneurs, however, struggle just as district leaders do to sidestep entrenched practices, raise funds, find talent, and secure support. Moreover, today's most successful ventures often pale when viewed beside the larger enterprise. The 70-odd KIPP schools, 150 principals trained annually by New Leaders for New Schools, and 4,800 teachers recruited each year by The New Teacher Project are dwarfed by the United States' 15,000 school districts, nearly 100,000 schools, and 3.3 million teachers. The questions are whether these creative problem solvers will ultimately make a real, lasting difference for millions of kids, and whether there are policies or practices that might increase the odds they will do so.

The Limits of the "Best Practices" Approach

For decades, the dominant approach to school improvement has emphasized what can be loosely termed "best practices." Advocates champion laws and instructional standards that promote familiar themes like curricular alignment, formative assessment, and professional development. The presumption is that improving schools and systems is primarily a matter of additional spending, measuring achievement, coaching educators, and applying additional expertise.[5] Best practice advocates presume that the right mix of remedies is already known—or will soon be identified—and that the challenge is primarily a technical one of program design, professional development, and implementation. At one level, this all makes good sense.

More telling, though, is that these well-intentioned efforts have consistently disappointed. Del Stover told this disheartening but familiar tale in the *American School Board Journal*:

> Five years ago, in a bid to boost achievement at Glades Central Community High School in Palm Beach County, Fla., officials promised smaller classes, more professional development for teachers, and curriculum changes. Two years ago, with student achievement still lagging, officials

promised even more support and greater oversight, and again assured the community that they knew how to fix Glades Central's problems. But saying you know what it takes to fix the problem and actually doing so are very different things.[6]

Indeed, Heather Driscoll, the founder of Revolutionary Schools, a New Hampshire–based firm that helps New England schools align curricula, resources, and policy, wearily notes, "We often find ourselves working to counteract a pervasive 'silver bullet' culture. The cycle is predictable. Schools attempt to rise to increasing expectations by employing innumerable silver bullet solutions. . . . Unfortunately, this tinkering occurs with little to no coordination between teachers, grades, and schools." Driscoll explains the problem is that best practices are repeatedly adopted with little or no coordination, and "systemic change is not something you can just photocopy and cheer on."

Several years ago, I headed up a yearlong effort to study the impact of Superintendent Alan Bersin's extended effort to radically reform the San Diego City Schools. At the end of the exercise, I was forced to grimly conclude the following:

> Perhaps the most important lesson from San Diego is how limited the possibilities are for radical improvement short of structural change to personnel systems, technology, accountability, leadership, and compensation. For all their sweat and struggle, Bersin and his team found their efforts to build a 21st century workforce checked by state law and contract language governing teacher hiring, school assignment, compensation, and work rules. An outdated information technology system meant that the district has been scrambling to develop the tools required for serious accountability, human resources, and budgeting improvements. Bersin began his tenure with considerable advantages, including his dazzling local and national contacts. . . . If the legacy of his seven-year run is in doubt, [it] illustrates, above all, the gauntlet that today awaits even the boldest school reformers.[7]

Pilot Lights That Keep Going Out

Schools and systems have tried to emulate the best practices of one heralded pilot site after another, and yet the hoped-for outcomes never seem to materialize at scale. It's a lot like repeatedly sparking a pilot light without ever getting the furnace to ignite. Disappointing results are inevitably chalked up to flawed implementation. In truth, the failure of most such efforts is due to barnacles that encumber today's school systems, including inefficient human resource departments, intrusive collective bargaining agreements, outdated technology, poorly designed management information systems, and other structural impediments. Greenfielders do not reject the utility of sensible best practices, but they question the assumption that the best practice mind-set will be enough to overcome these obstacles—and express doubt that best practices can prove fully effective, given the shape of today's school systems, colleges of education, and educational ecosystem.

An instructive case in the limits of best practice reform is Deborah Meier's disheartening experience with the famed Central Park East Secondary School in New York City. Featuring a challenging and coherent best-practice vision of a personalized, inquiry-driven school, Central Park East enjoyed notable success with a disadvantaged population and received national acclaim. A decade later, Meier left to launch a second school in Boston. Before long, Central Park East lost many of her handpicked staff and saw its distinctive approach diluted. By 2005, Meier noted, "I stopped visiting. It was too painful."[8] Absent the constant, hands-on attention of a remarkable leader like Meier, "model" schools and districts can quickly backslide. The result is a stylized dance, with dynamic reformers enjoying some success tackling troubled schools in this or that community only to see the problems re-emerge when attention, resources, and energy shift elsewhere.

The sad truth is that while individual schools have successfully produced superior results (at least for a while), best practice reform has never delivered an example of successfully transforming a mediocre school system into a high-performing one. There are a number of highly respected suburban districts we can point to, such as Montgomery County, Maryland, or Fairfax County, Virginia, but these systems inevitably start with the advantages conferred by educated, relatively affluent, and education-conscious parents and community members. Meanwhile, touted examples of urban reform such as those in Charlotte, Boston, and Austin deserve their due, but Stanford professor emeritus Larry Cuban has sardonically wondered whether these efforts are "as good as it gets."[9] The reality is that these acclaimed districts are impressive only relative to their peers. In terms of student learning, achievement, or attainment, even proponents concede that these districts have a long way to go. If we are to deliver transformative improvement, it is not enough to wedge new practices into familiar schools and districts; we must re-imagine the system itself.

Of Technology and Silver Bullets

The troubled record of best practice reform is often accompanied by a false faith in "silver bullets." The history of education technology provides an excellent illustration of this phenomenon. Decade after decade, fanciful new best practices have often advanced in tandem with the promise that buying televisions or computers, linking to the Internet, providing students with laptops, or incorporating whiteboards will finally be *the thing* that delivers dramatic improvement in teaching and learning. It has long been noticed, as Cuban observed in *Oversold and Underused*, that the potential of technology has persistently gone unfulfilled, with film projectors, televisions, computers, and the Internet simply a series of expensive baubles shoveled into otherwise unchanged schools and classrooms.[10]

In their recent book, *Liberating Learning*, EdisonLearning executive John Chubb and Stanford University professor Terry Moe make the case that new technologies have the potential to transform the politics of education and rewrite the rules governing system routines. They argue that new technologies are marked by characteristics—including geographic dispersion, individualization, transparency, the expansion of choices, and organic evolution—that will alter traditional power relationships and weaken or break through political and organizational barriers.[11] Harvard Business School professor Clayton Christensen has sounded similar notes in his buzzed-about volume *Disrupting Class*, arguing that the cost-efficiency and flexibility of Web-based instruction will cause it to increasingly displace, and not merely augment, the traditional classroom experience.[12] Whatever the response to these particular analyses, the larger point is that harnessing the transformative power of technology demands a profoundly different approach from the "supplement, not supplant" tack that has long held sway.

Whereas best practice reformers believe the solution lies in new instructional strategies and improved coaching, a greenfielder believes the practices, rules, and routines that have proven so resistant to change must first be peeled away. Yet, while it is foolhardy to expect new programs or extra training to overcome the hurdles posed by the existing system, the failure of technology to revolutionize teaching and learning has been frequently (and mistakenly) understood not as an indictment of our system of schooling but as evidence that the transformative power of technology somehow stops at the schoolhouse door.

Best practice advocates have regularly imported a variety of advances from outside K–12 education. But by the time these have been pasteurized to suit the political and organizational realities of schooling, they typically emerge as fads rather than meaningful new initiatives. The four steps of this process are familiar. First, reformers seize upon simple, powerful intuitions from the world of management—notions like decentralization or talent competition. Second, they wrap these ideas in trendy jargon that makes them sound new, renders them safe for educational consumption, and obscures their harsh edges. Thus, we get excited talk of "site-based management" or "human capital development," with little attention to why these strategies are effective or what it takes to make them work. Third, these proposals are partially and often incoherently pursued in a manner that does not unduly disturb existing practices. Finally, when the results inevitably disappoint, we decide the notion itself was flawed and set off in search of a new silver bullet.

How Greenfield Differs from Best Practices

The greenfield perspective is profoundly different from the best practice mind-set. It questions whether the right mix of approaches is as self-evident, straightforward, or universally applicable as imagined. Even when the familiar recipes are the right ones, or when other promising strategies are identified, greenfielders question whether existing systems are capable of using them effectively or for a sustained period and fear that best practice proponents underestimate the difficulty of overhauling troubled organizations.

Whereas public districts require officials to force change through resistant bureaucracies, or expect individual teachers and principals to freelance within indifferent organizations, greenfielders create room for entrepreneurs to build new organizations focused on addressing clearly articulated problems, for example, The New Teacher Project helping districts recruit talented candidates in areas of critical need or Catapult Learning delivering tutoring to underperforming students. When freed from encumbrances, such ventures can rapidly extend successful services to vast numbers of students, teachers, schools, or districts in multiple jurisdictions. In other words, in lieu of efforts to reform each of the country's 15,000 school districts, a single entrepreneurial venture might dramatically improve instruction, teacher recruitment, data analysis, or school management across hundreds or thousands of districts.

Greenfielders trust in the ingenuity of talented, motivated individuals—*if, and only if,* those individuals are in an environment conducive to success, are responsible for the quality of their work, and are able to tap into crucial capital, talent, and support. This means the key work for policymakers is not only to clear away impediments but also to create the conditions for entrepreneurial success. The key work for researchers is to develop the ideas that entrepreneurs will harness. The key work for those with intriguing ideas or boutique programs is to demonstrate that their vision and products can serve thousands and then millions. This is, needless to say, a much less exalted role than the best practice approach typically accords to policymakers and researchers or that best practice gurus typically see themselves playing.

The greenfield strategy is both more modest and more ambitious than the best practice approach. It is more modest in that it does not imagine that we will "fix" our schools in the next few years—or the next few decades—but instead regards school improvement as an uneven, ongoing project and embraces the Confucian adage that a journey of a thousand miles begins with a single step. It is more ambitious in that it does not merely seek to improve schools but envisions the continuous emergence of profoundly better ways to deliver and support teaching and learning.

Why Greenfield Reform Is Safer Than It May Seem

Today, our schools confront challenges that our education system was not designed and is not equipped to meet. Erected haphazardly over more than a century, it was configured to process large numbers of students in a 20th century industrial nation. These arrangements once sufficed, but they are no longer adequate given worldwide employment trends and the demands of a knowledge-based economy. Meanwhile, decades of attempted systemic reforms have yielded the frustrating results reflected by book titles like David Tyack and Larry Cuban's iconic *Tinkering Toward Utopia* or my own *Spinning Wheels.*[13]

Greenfield entails uncertainty—something we instinctively shrink from when discussing children. In weighing that concern, it is helpful to keep three things in mind. First, all risks are not created equal. Having a school abruptly close midyear may be an unacceptable risk, but more teacher turnover or mediocre tutoring providers may be less problematic. Second, there are many ways to limit uncertainty and promote vigorous, smart quality control, which we will address later. Third, if "risk" refers to the likelihood that schools will leave children ill-served, thousands of today's schools are terribly risky; the question is whether we can find ways to do better without creating unnecessary new problems.

We routinely overlook the perils implicit in the status quo. Editorial Projects in Education has calculated that the U.S. national graduation rate today is only 73 percent.[14] In urban districts, the graduation rate is just 60 percent,[15] while major cities like Dallas, Denver, Indianapolis, Milwaukee, Detroit, Oakland, and Philadelphia fail to graduate even half of their students.[16] On average, black students graduate high school with math and reading scores that are four grade levels behind those of whites, and U.S. students generally lag on reputable international assessments, such as the Programme for International Student Assessment (PISA) and Trends in International Mathematics and Science Study (TIMMS).[17] Standing pat is hardly a comfortable option.

Nonetheless, today's educational leaders—enmeshed in bureaucracy, governed by elected representatives, and scrutinized by anxious parents and civic leaders—shy away from disruptive change. The University of Washington's Paul Hill has argued that overly restrictive provisions in collective bargaining agreements have meant that district and school leaders have "virtually lost the ability to choose teachers, make work assignments, fire ineffective teachers, and manage budgets."[18] The legal reform group Common Good has catalogued the statutes and regulations governing public high schools in New York City and identified more than 60 separate sources of rules and procedures with which administrators must comply, such as the 83 steps required to terminate an ineffective teacher.[19]

One tiny but powerful illustration of such challenges can be found in Washington, DC—specifically in District of Columbia Public Schools (DCPS) chancellor Michelle Rhee's experience promoting a pilot initiative to facilitate parental involvement. Part of her efforts involved making information on student performance, including attendance data, more readily accessible to parents. Rhee wanted teachers to begin taking attendance on computers, so that this data could be instantly downloaded and available online later the same day. The district's regular process would have meant a week or more before data could be posted. A sticking point quickly emerged: the DCPS collective bargaining agreement specifically obligated teachers to take attendance but also prohibited the district leadership from requiring them to do data entry—and taking attendance on a laptop instead of on paper could be deemed to constitute data entry. Multiply that tiny incident by a thousand similar stumbling blocks, and one quickly understands how daunting it is to reengineer a district barnacled with contracts, protocols, ingrained norms, and veteran staff, who may be resistant to reinvention.

Entrepreneurship is necessary precisely because organizations are reluctant to upset established routines and because leaders who seek to do so are hampered by a wealth of obstacles, large and small. The remedy is Schumpeter's "creative destruction" and the opportunity for new ventures to emerge, challenge, and displace the old. A greenfielder believes that the risks of inaction far outweigh those posed by quality-conscious entrepreneurship.

Why Greenfield Schooling Is Necessary

When it comes to this whole notion of educational entrepreneurship, a natural instinct is to read the preceding discussion but still wonder, "Is all this really necessary? This sounds far removed from improving instruction and student engagement—can't we find a straightforward solution?" Experience suggests that the answer is no.

Progress is messy, in part because workable solutions change over time. What worked in the 1950s may not prove as effective in the 2010s. Indeed, in the 2006 volume *Economic Turbulence*, Clair Brown, John Haltiwanger, and Julia Lane observe that the average life span of a Fortune 500 company—from its conception to its disappearance—is only 50 years.[20] And these are the most successful firms in the world. Just think about that for a moment. Most Fortune 500 companies erected before 1950 are no longer with us. Meanwhile, almost every school system in the United States already existed in 1950, and most are the direct descendants of organizations that took shape more than a century ago.

Even more daunting is the idea that we must devise improvement strategies that can be imposed across more than 15,000 districts and in nearly 100,000 schools. Educators do not always realize what a staggering goal this represents. There is not a single sector where widespread efforts across hundreds or thousands of organizations have resulted in dramatic gains in quality. Radical improvement is more commonly the product of new entrants solving a problem with a particular strategy, and then building an organization that can deliver the breakthrough to a vast population.

If Apple, Amazon, eBay, or Pixar were to operate like today's K–12 districts, they would not deliver their products or services to millions of users. Instead, Amazon would serve the greater Seattle area, and imitators from across the country would flock to the Pacific Northwest, learn Amazon's secrets, and return home to emulate its practices. Expansion would be slow and uneven, many imitators would adopt "best practices" without the talent or focus to execute them properly, and reams of studies would seek to explain Amazon's secrets so that other communities could reliably order books online. Consider, though, that once Amazon devised a viable model, no one thought it necessary for policymakers to entice others to mimic its success; we simply trusted that opportunity and the prospect of rewards would spur an effort to deliver the service as widely as possible. Rather than our repeated efforts to reinvent the wheel in district after district, constantly seeking to bring the mountain to Mohammed, we may fare better by focusing on how we might allow and encourage problem solvers to take their services to a wealth of communities and kids.

The Turnaround Mirage

Some would-be reformers have responded to the disappointing track record of best practice reform by latching onto dramatic proposals for restructuring and "turnarounds." There is cause for caution in relying too heavily on such strategies, however. While "turnarounds" are relatively novel in schooling, they have been a staple of business management for decades. The hope and energy invested in turnaround efforts in other sectors have generally yielded only mixed results. Consulting firms Arthur D. Little and McKinsey & Company have studied implementation of Total Quality Management at hundreds of companies and have determined that about two-thirds fall short of their hoped-for results.[21] Despite the passion, money, and expertise thrown into organizational change, most turnaround initiatives fail to deliver. Leaders of the similarly dramatic "corporate reengineering movement" have reported that the success rate for Fortune 1000 companies is below 50 percent and possibly as low as 20 percent.[22]

Even in the private sector, where management enjoys many more degrees of freedom and where competition can lend a sense of urgency, turnarounds are an iffy proposition. Peter Senge, director of the Center for Organizational Learning at the MIT Sloan School of Management, has observed, "Failure to sustain significant change recurs again and again despite substantial resources committed to the change effort . . . talented and committed people 'driving the change,' and high stakes."[23] Even when everyone agrees change is essential, it is enormously difficult to upend established institutions.

Why It's Hard for Elephants to Dance

In sector after sector, solving new problems—or more effectively addressing old ones—has been the province of new entrants. There is a reason that IBM, for all its resources and muscle in the 1980s, was not able to provide access to personal computing in the way that its new competitors could. An IBM sales force built around selling giant machines to corporations with hands-on customer service was not positioned to compete with Michael Dell selling hand-assembled personal computers through the mail. Similarly, legacy airlines like Pan Am, with their pricey jets and top-heavy workforce, floundered as upstarts like Southwest and JetBlue emerged and prospered.

For all their resources, these corporate giants had to wrestle with the handicaps imposed by their success. Size, habit, and an established position left them lumbering and heavy footed. While young, they built processes, metrics, and hiring and compensation systems in accordance with their needs and the norms of the day. As they got larger, they were equipped to keep doing the same thing but stumbled when technologies, management practices, or consumer demands changed. The tendency of successful firms to become trapped by their own success is what Harvard Business School professor Clayton Christensen termed the "innovator's dilemma" more than a decade ago.[24] Established organizations do well by sticking to the models and practices that have gotten them where they are. This makes them lousy at addressing changing needs, tapping new pools of talent, or harnessing new technologies.

Meanwhile, new organizations—freed from a rigid mentality about how things should be done—crop up, take advantage of new opportunities, and more nimbly tackle looming challenges. Just 40 years ago, today's ubiquitous titans like Wal-Mart and McDonald's were hungry, young companies. Other household names, like MTV and Starbucks, didn't even exist. Eventually, the nimble and successful organizations of one era become the hidebound institutions of the next, as the practices that made them successful become hardwired and difficult to change. Attuned to the human resources, technology, opportunities, and needs of a particular landscape, once-envied organizations eventually find themselves at a disadvantage as that landscape changes, and new entrants seize upon new tools, technologies, opportunities, and changes in the workforce. The price of success is that yesterday's entrepreneurs come to wrestle with the same sorts of problems that once made them necessary, in a continuous cycle of birth, growth, decay, and regeneration.

Best practice reformers turn a blind eye to a crucial challenge of innovation, which is often not surfacing a new solution but mustering the will and capacity to implement it faithfully. For instance, watching General Motors and Chrysler stumble into bankruptcy in 2008 and 2009, one might have thought their problems were new or unforeseen. In fact, these companies had recognized the need to unwind their onerous labor agreements, control exorbitant labor costs, escape unaffordable pension plans, and downsize dealer networks since at least the 1980s. However, the combination of strong unions, worker expectations, a lack of urgency, and a desire to avoid messy conflict led corporate leaders to repeatedly kick the can down the road, even as GM's and Chrysler's market shares continued to shrink. Only under the shadow of bankruptcy and direct pressure from the U.S. government did these firms find the gumption to attempt previously unthinkable changes.

Similarly, consider the fate of the newspaper industry. Starting in the 1990s, analysts observed that the Internet posed a death threat to the traditional newspaper business model and argued that companies had to exploit the new technology aggressively to reduce costs and rethink their routines. As columnist Michael Kinsley has wryly observed, "If you had told one of the great newspaper moguls of the past that someday it would be possible to publish a newspaper without paying anything for paper, printing, and delivery, he would not have predicted that this would mean catastrophe for the industry."[25] Newspapers largely dismissed critiques of their coverage and concerns about their viability, continuing to operate pretty much as they always had, while tacking on Web operations and giving away their content online. That approach worked fine—for a time. Then, entrepreneurial ventures like Daily

Kos, the Huffington Post, and the Drudge Report increasingly figured out how to seize the new opportunities presented by the Internet greenfield.

The traditional media scrambled to catch up while struggling to slough off the burdensome costs imposed by established contracts, large staffs, printing facilities, and delivery trucks that once reflected their success but now weighed them down. Coverage on the collapse of the newspaper industry focused on the costs, but emerging organizations are not only recreating some of what is being lost but devising new ways to use the technology to create communities, solicit feedback, promote accountability, and boost the relevance and accessibility—and potentially the quality—of coverage. As Kinsley has noted, "If General Motors goes under, there will still be cars. And if the *New York Times* disappears, there will still be news."[26] Keep in mind that Schumpeter's "creative destruction" is as much about creation as about destruction. The disappearance of the old may elicit nostalgia, but it also frees up the resources and talent that can pave the way for new advances.

Schools occupy a more privileged place than the automakers or the newspapers. Providing a public good and funded by public taxes, they know their revenue stream is not going to dry up. For all the vague talk about how schools must change, and change now, automakers were able to hold off the tide for three decades, and newspapers for 15 years. How long can schools stave off change? The honest truth is they can probably sit fast for many years to come, but whose interests would it serve to do so? Retooling schools will doubtless be uncomfortable for many adults, but it is the right thing to do for the students. A greenfielder insists that we devote our energy not to holding the fort but to embracing transformation.

The Role of the Entrepreneur

Entrepreneurs devise better solutions and build organizations to deliver these solutions to thousands and then millions of people, upsetting the reigning titans. They are the men and women who launch the FedExes and Googles and make routine what was once deemed impossible, whether that's shipping a package anywhere on Earth in a day or tapping humanity's accumulated knowledge in a fraction of a second.

Today's school systems do not attract entrepreneurs. After all, educators and educational leaders are not selected for their ability to conceive of radically new ideas or build new organizations. That is no surprise, as this is not the work they are asked to do; they are typically selected to serve as stewards of long-standing and relatively stable organizations.

When it comes to understanding just what skills and traits an entrepreneur requires, there is cause to be wary of sweeping generalizations. But successful entrepreneurs do generally exhibit a broad set of common traits. Bryan Hassel of Public Impact has identified six key traits that these individuals tend to share:

- *A Need for Achievement* and a tendency to set high goals and pursue them relentlessly, with clear metrics for success.
- *An Urgent Approach to Problem-Solving* in which they relentlessly seek out solutions, trying and discarding failed strategies.
- *An Internal Locus of Control* in which they deem themselves as responsible for the outcomes of their actions and are unwilling to make excuses for failure.
- *A Tolerance for Ambiguity* and a powerful ability to flexibly adapt as conditions warrant.
- *A Preference for Strategic Influencing.* Though they may have strong interpersonal skills, they focus less on cultivating long-term relationships and more on using personal relationships to address immediate organizational needs.
- *A Bias for Action through Organization-Building.* As Smith and Petersen have written, "[Entrepreneurs'] sense of urgency and drive to achieve leads them to take action by creating new organizations that will make their vision a reality."[27]

Entrepreneurs have the chutzpah and hubris to take on daunting projects, with the conviction that they have the determination and talent to succeed. As Wendy Kopp, who founded Teach For America in 1989 as a newly minted Princeton graduate, has noted, "Many people could not accept that a young woman with no real-world experience could possibly run such an ambitious, untested enterprise."[28]

Education Entrepreneurs Don't Just Start Schools

Educational entrepreneurs serve a variety of needs. They seek to teach children who have been ill-served, improve the quality of educators and school leaders, provide more effective tools to educators, and deliver services in more useful and accessible ways. In short, they tackle the same problems as other educators; the difference is in how they go about it. These entrepreneurial types can be grouped into three broad categories.

The best-known entrepreneurs are those who launch new schools and networks of schools. These *school builders* include a variety of charter management organizations and "mom and pop" efforts and include such well-known ventures as the National Heritage Academies, High Tech High School, and the Green Dot Public Schools. Contrary to a common misperception, not all entrepreneurs are in the business of opening new schools. A second group of organizations are *talent providers*, focused on improving the quality of instruction and leadership by finding more promising ways to recruit, develop, and support teachers and school leaders. A third set of ventures is composed of *tool builders* and *service providers*—entrepreneurs who provide distance learning, instructional devices, data systems, curricula, educational programs, or other services that leverage technology or research.

Many Flavors of Education Entrepreneurs

In the 2009 report Stimulating Excellence, Public Impact analysts Bryan Hassel and Julie Kowal classify three general categories of entrepreneurs and offer several examples of each. They highlight entrepreneurs who open charter schools, those who attract or cultivate talent, and those who provide a variety of services to families or schools.

Charter schools. Aspire Public Schools operates charter schools in California, with an emphasis on serving low-income communities. In 2008, Aspire served more than 6,000 students in 21 schools throughout the state. The Knowledge Is Power Program (KIPP), the largest nonprofit charter school network, operates 66 schools based on the same fundamental model in 19 states and Washington, DC. Smaller clusters of schools are also emerging through charter management organizations (CMOs) such as Ascend Learning, based in New York City. Ascend opened its first college-preparatory elementary school in 2008 and plans to open a second school in 2009. The MATCH middle and high schools follow a rigorous college-preparatory focus and serve approximately 300 students in two schools located in the Boston area.

Human capital builders. New Leaders for New Schools (NLNS) recruits and trains individuals to become principals in both charter and district-run schools in high-need urban areas. Over 400 New Leaders currently lead schools in disadvantaged communities across the country. Teach For America (TFA) has mobilized 20,000 of the nation's most successful college graduates to close the achievement gap in underserved urban and rural schools across the United States. The New Teacher

Project (TNTP) partners with school districts to recruit, train, select, and hire high-quality teachers, often from non-traditional routes. TNTP also works with school districts to improve their human resources systems. New Schools for New Orleans, a nonprofit created to build the supply of high-quality schools in the aftermath of Hurricane Katrina, helps launch new charter schools; works with NLNS, TNTP, TFA, and other entrepreneurial organizations to attract and prepare teachers for New Orleans schools; and supports advocacy on behalf of public education in New Orleans.

Service providers. Citizen Schools operates a high-quality, hands-on after-school program and apprenticeships for 6th, 7th, and 8th grade students in seven states across the country. College Summit provides schools, districts, and colleges with strategies and tools to build their capacity to increase the number of students who go to college. K12 Inc. operates full-time virtual public schools in several states and provides a custom curriculum and learning tools for traditional and homeschool instruction. SchoolNet provides real-time data, reports, tools, and content to help teachers, schools, and districts assess students' reading progress and individualize instruction. Wireless Generation markets educational technology that allows teachers to monitor students' progress using handheld computers that enable them to analyze data and customize their instruction to students' needs. GreatSchools.net, an online database and Web community, provides parents and policymakers with data and reviews of every public school in the United States. [29]

How Entrepreneurs Serve the Larger System

As Smith and Petersen have noted, entrepreneurs are currently playing three key roles when it comes to school improvement.[30] The first is the role of change agent. Entrepreneurs can demonstrate what is possible when resources are used differently and point the way toward sensible changes in policy and practice. For example, Teach For America has directly touched more than 20,000 recruits and the millions of students whom those teachers have taught, but TFA's greater impact has been reshaping the perception of teaching and the strategies used to recruit and prepare teachers.

Second, entrepreneurs can attract other individuals with skills and mind-sets that are often scarce in K–12 schooling. Entrepreneurial organizations appeal to achievement-oriented employees who might otherwise be repelled by the more bureaucratic workings of public education. These employees develop results-based cultures while sacrificing the security of employment guarantees and seniority-based progression. "I have all the agility in the world—and I have nobody to blame but myself if I don't succeed," explains

Larry Rosenstock, the former carpenter/lawyer/professor/principal-turned-entrepreneur whom we met earlier in the chapter.[31]

A third contribution of entrepreneurs is to create laboratories for experimentation. As problem solvers, entrepreneurs are constantly learning, reviewing progress and correcting course. While this is what we hope districts and schools will do, it is far easier for entrepreneurial organizations to develop new practices. For instance, Green Dot Public Schools, a charter school organization launched in Los Angeles in 1999 by novelist and political activist Steve Barr, has pioneered a "thin contract" that serves as a much more flexible, less bureaucratic alternative to the conventional labor agreement. This kind of experiment is far more difficult, if not impossible, to execute within the existing routines and machinery in most districts.

The Key Role of District and State Leaders

The discussion thus far might seem to imply that greenfield schooling happens outside the purview of traditional districts and thus has little to do with today's state and district leaders. Nothing could be farther from the truth. As Columbia University Teachers College professor Jeffrey Henig has explained, the dominance of laws and public funds over K–12 education means that public officials will always set the boundaries when it comes to reinventing schooling.[32] Creating greenfield depends crucially on the willingness of state and district officials to sow opportunities for new ventures to take root and thrive. Lack of interest or opposition will not entirely squelch these ventures but will surely stifle their emergence and retard their growth. Building a better mousetrap is irrelevant if states or districts won't permit it to be sold.

Ultimately, the promise of High Tech High School, Green Dot, Ascend Learning, and many other ventures like them rests on the actions of school, district, and state officials. Matt Candler, hired in 2001 as KIPP's first vice president of school development, offers a telling anecdote on this count.[33] Candler was charged with equipping school leaders to open up new campuses across the country. He recalls that local efforts to ensure funding, facilities, and school autonomy were the key to expansion. Candler explains, "It was easy to train blazers [KIPP staff tasked with "trailblazing" the way for new schools] on how to diagnose the fiscal and facilities landscape in a city, but teaching folks to have a good read on the freedom we needed was harder. We were looking for congruence, especially between those folks who wanted us in town and those who were going to be our bosses—the state and district staffers or board members who authorized and oversaw charter schools. Our first all-blazer road trip illustrates how important diagnosing freedom was to KIPP."

He recalls, "In late 2001, the blazers all flew into Atlanta. . . . Our destination was Thomasville, Georgia." KIPP enthusiasts, including Georgia Governor Roy Barnes, had lobbied the superintendent, and KIPP was on the Thomasville school board agenda for that afternoon. Candler notes, "In Georgia, the local board had to approve any new school for it to receive full funding, and we wanted a unanimous affirmation of KIPP from the board. We walked the superintendent through our presentation, and he explained that we might meet some resistance in the school board."

Candler remembers that, at 5:00 p.m., "We filed into the board room behind Marni [Mohr, a member of the KIPP team]. She delivered a flawless explanation of KIPP and explained what the foundation would do to support a new KIPP school in Thomasville. She finished up and asked for questions. She got nothing. Not a question. Not a single comment. No 'Thank you,' no 'No thank you.' Marni would summarize the situation later: 'Crickets. I could hear crickets chirping outside.'"

KIPP did not open a school in Thomasville, Candler notes, but the organization learned a great lesson. He explains, "The authorizer—in this case, the district itself—had little interest in KIPP, much less in new schools as a vehicle for change in its system. . . . If leadership in a city really wanted KIPP to be a part of their reform agenda, they had to invest in making sure the people who would actually approve schools—the authorizers and those who run the system day-to-day—were on the same page and valued new high-quality school creation. That was not the case in Thomasville."

K–12 schooling is not like computer software or dry cleaning, where the central question is whether an entrepreneur can devise a good product, convince customers to buy it, and outmaneuver competitors. Instead, it is fused with thorny questions of public policy, the public weal, social justice, and public outlays. The ability of greenfield ventures to thrive therefore depends heavily on state officials, local school districts, and regulations. Why should those officials want to be helpful? What can they do to be helpful? Those are among the questions this book will tackle.

What About Democratic Education?

Some critics worry that greenfield schooling is somehow at odds with the democratic values enshrined in public education or that it is a recipe for inequity. In truth, it is the existing industrial-age model of schooling that is most problematic for urban and rural students, and it is in these locales that abandoning the standardized, bureaucratic model holds the most promise for students and educators. Such a shift is entirely compatible with the traditions of American democracy. As University of Washington professor Paul Hill has argued, "A Jeffersonian version of democracy . . . expects arrangements to be temporary, and institutions to be re-thought fundamentally as times and needs change."[34] Greenfield proceeds from the premise that such a Jeffersonian vision is both true to democratic principles and suited to the challenges of our age.

Some greenfield skeptics have argued that increasing the role of private nonprofits or for-profits in schooling is a de facto retreat from public schooling. In fact, even champions of free markets like John Stuart Mill and Milton Friedman have recognized that education is a public good as well as a private one, and have argued for state funding. Mill even called for state testing to ensure that all children are adequately served. However, stipulating a public role in funding and overseeing quality should not dictate how teaching and learning are provided. Legislators routinely craft policies intended to address various public needs but rely upon both public agencies and private firms to execute them. In such cases, we generally accept that a public service is being rendered regardless of who provides it.

After all, in the United States, the Social Security Administration, the Environmental Protection Agency, the Department of Education, and just about every other government agency contracts with private firms to provide public services and pursue public goals. We are still comfortable asserting that these institutions are serving public ends because providers are paid with public dollars, monitored by public agencies, and directed by public designs. In education, for-profit firms have long provided school districts with everything from textbooks to facilities, and few have suggested that this practice is problematic. So it is unclear why allowing new school builders, tool builders, or talent providers to play a larger role is threatening, so long as the state is providing for the education of all students and providers are held accountable in sensible ways.

There are also critics who deem it morally problematic that some new ventures are for-profit. The logic behind this assertion is a bit murky. For one thing, we have a long tradition of for-profit ventures supplying pencils, desks, computers, professional development, and a host of other products and services to schools. For another, as scholars have noted, "It is almost a paradox of American culture that we applaud entrepreneurs who make their fortune with frivolous products, such as the 'Pet Rock,' but chastise those who would make the same profit . . . trying to make the world a better place."[35]

From an Industrial to an Entrepreneurial Society

Rather than wonder whether we can justify a greenfield approach to schooling, the real question is whether we can make the case for clinging to our industrial-era systems. Not only have traditional reform stratagems fallen short, but they are also increasingly ill-suited for a sector at the heart of a knowledge economy. The system of schooling that emerged from the Common School Movement and the Progressive Era, whatever its merits once were, is no longer equal to meeting contemporary demands.

At the same time, a sweeping technological and managerial revolution has reordered society, creating opportunities and unleashing tools simply unimaginable a half-century ago. Indeed, Obama administration economic guru and former Harvard University president Lawrence Summers has suggested that "the world is experiencing the third biggest economic revolution of the past millennium alongside the Renaissance and the Industrial Revolution."[36]

"At any given time," Carl Schramm, president of the Ewing Marion Kauffman Foundation, has observed, "15 percent of the [U.S.] population is running their own companies"; these entrepreneurs "now create more than half the new jobs in America," and "we now live in the most entrepreneurial time in history."[37] Today, nearly half a million new U.S. businesses are created each month; new firms are now launched more frequently than babies are born![38]

In the 1970s, the popular face of commercial success was provided by the veteran heads of America's unrivaled corporate giants like General Motors, TWA, and AT&T. In the 1990s, that changed. Today, a similar gallery of icons would feature those who built successful ventures from scratch—figures like Bill Gates, Michael Dell, and Steve Jobs.

Dramatic advances in technology, transportation, and data storage have created new possibilities for autonomy, decentralization, and customization. In 1993, the Internet as we know it did not exist, and the U.S. Census Bureau reported that just 23 percent of the nation's households owned a personal computer; by 2003, when these data were most recently collected, 62 percent did.[39] In 2008, 25 states had established a virtual school, and every state had established curricular standards that included technology.[40] The iPod didn't exist in 2000; by the end of 2008, more than 173 million had been sold.[41] In short, a technological revolution has swept through U.S. homes and schools, creating new opportunities for communication, instruction, and operations.

The Book from Here

While it feels like a call for dramatic change (and it is), the defining characteristic of greenfield schooling is a profound humility deeply rooted in American traditions of pluralism, invention, and enterprise. A greenfielder does not presume that we know how to meet any of our pressing educational challenges—only that we should be skeptical of silver bullets and best practices, strip away formal and informal barriers that impede entrepreneurs, devise quality control and accountability systems, and find ways to provide the talent and resources that new ventures require.

Just as effective schools will not miraculously emerge without careful attention to instruction, curriculum, and leadership, so dynamic problem solvers will not serendipitously emerge in a risk-averse, bureaucratic sector or without attention to opportunity, accountability, talent, and resources. Chapter 2, "Tilling the Field," explains what it means to create greenfield and sketches the broad dimensions of what such efforts entail. Chapter 3, "Barriers," discusses the first, essential step of removing the formal and informal impediments that trip up entrepreneurs. Chapter 4, "Quality," addresses the need to focus on performance and to hold new and old providers accountable for the caliber and cost-effectiveness of their work, while ensuring that accountability enables, rather than stifles, creative problem solving. Chapter 5, "Talent," notes that the single most important resource for fertile greenfield is an abundance of human capital. Chapter 6, "Money," addresses the other key ingredient for new ventures: where entrepreneurs get capital and how support can fuel energetic problem solving. Finally, Chapter 7, "Getting Started," offers some guidance for educators, policymakers, philanthropists, and reformers, sketching principles that can help ensure that 21st century schooling becomes the creative, dynamic space that it can and should be. To begin, let us turn to the question of just what it means to cultivate greenfield.

2

TILLING THE FIELD

THE GREENFIELD APPROACH regards school improvement as something that policymakers and advocates *enable* rather than *do*. In his 1974 Nobel Prize acceptance lecture "The Pretence of Knowledge," Austrian economist Friedrich von Hayek famously urged policymakers to emulate gardeners rather than engineers and to create the environment for growth rather than to pursue it directly. Hayek argued that trial and error, feedback loops, and competition more often surface good solutions to thorny social problems than do officials and experts devising grand fixes from their elevated perch. If decades of fads and bouts of disappointing reforms have done nothing else, they have made a powerful case for such humility in schooling.

Hesitant to take risks when dealing with children, reformers of every ideological stripe prefer to champion solutions that minimize uncertainty. Thus, the most popular reforms often are the costly and typically ineffectual but otherwise "risk-free" options like smaller class sizes or increased professional development. This mind-set is reflected even in celebrated "innovative" programs, such as the $5 billion that Congress authorized in 2009 for the U.S. secretary of education's "Race to the Top" and "Investing in What Works & Innovation" funds. While earmarked to promote innovation, these dollars have been targeted primarily to support such unobjectionable measures as improving state standards and data systems. The initiative is an interesting one, and certainly the two programs represent a potentially welcome departure from federal funding formulas. Nonetheless, the guidelines that have recently emerged from the Department of Education have emphasized compliance with federal guidelines on teacher pay and charter schooling rather than rewarding states for their own creative problem solving. What to make of the programs, however, will become clear only in the fullness of time. The distaste for entrepreneurial risk in schooling, however, reflects a failure to frankly consider how progress unfolds elsewhere in the world.

The Rigors of Getting Started

Celine Coggins is the executive director for Teach Plus, an organization seeking to encourage new educators to stay in teaching by expanding leadership opportunities and financial incentives for those who demonstrate classroom success. Founded in 2008, Teach Plus currently works in Boston and Indianapolis. "I'm launching an organization to address an issue that no district, school, or outside organization addresses well—teacher retention. But in launching an organization in a space that doesn't currently exist . . . there's so much to do and there aren't a lot of good roadmaps," Coggins explains. "I'm learning it on the ground as I go."

Coggins's experience makes clear just how tough entrepreneurship always is, but also how it's in our power to make that work harder or easier. "There have been multiple stages where the trick is just lining up three things," she says. "One is the work, two is the staff, and three is the funding. Those pieces all have to come together in some kind of synergy that seems almost impossible to attain. For example, I reached one threshold back in the fall when I got both The Mind Trust fellowship and funding from NewSchools Venture Fund [we'll discuss both in Chapter 6] literally in the same day. . . . I think they must have both been looking at each other in a game of chicken: 'We're going to fund her if you fund her.'" So Coggins found herself almost on pause, waiting for one or the other to move first.

She says, "One thing I underestimated is the depth of relationships you need with funders. . . . I started having conversations with national funders about this work more than a year ago that are only now close to panning out. But it's been over the course of a year of them saying, 'We really like what you're doing. Let's just see you move the ball forward 10 more yards. Ten more yards!' And so each time I call them and say, 'Look what we've done. We've moved the ball forward 10 more yards!' And then they say, 'All right, just 10 more yards!'"

She notes an important consequence: "I have four or five people who are extraordinary in terms of their capacity to do the work. But I'm stuck stringing them along all in various ways, telling them, 'We're going to need to [move quickly], as soon as a couple of big funders say they want us doing this work in more cities than just Indianapolis and Boston.' And so . . . another [piece] is just the magic synergy that has to happen between getting the work going in the different cities, getting the staff, and getting the funding. I didn't understand that the timing around that is incredibly complex."

Coggins offers a particularly telling example of the multiple headaches entrepreneurs endure. She explains, "Our Web site is currently 'teach-plus.org.'

We've been in an international, escalating war to get 'teachplus.org' for over six months." That domain name is owned by a man in Finland who, Coggins notes, "does not have a strong command of the English language or an interest in actually using the site." She goes on: "There are six months of correspondence between us that start with him telling me I can have the site for free and then retracting the offer. . . . [This] slowed us down for months in getting e-mail addresses and getting our Web site up."

Coggins mentions another challenge typical for young entrepreneurs: "I have an idea that I really believe in and I'm willing to do whatever it takes to see it succeed, [but] I have a limited track record in entrepreneurship and in organizational leadership. I've had to go way over my own head to build a senior leadership team. . . . So now Teach Plus has three senior staff. Though I'm the one who formally leads the organization and owns all of the biggest headaches, I am the lowest paid by far." She smiles, "I would never have expected to found and run an organization and be the least [well] paid [member] on its staff!"

We Can't Always Predict What Will Work

Empowering entrepreneurs is not a safe or sure bet. Much that works in a given school will not be easy to bring to scale, and even carefully planned efforts can come up short. New solutions are inevitably going to involve trial and error. Harvard Business School professor Clayton Christensen, author of *The Innovator's Solution*, has reported that more than 90 percent of all successful new businesses wind up employing a strategy other than the one the founders initially adopted.[1]

A persistent stumbling block is that our imaginations are limited by what we have already seen. Chris Whittle, founder of Edison Schools (now EdisonLearning), has observed, "There was a time in aviation when the propeller was the only way to move a plane forward. Designers could not envision getting beyond a certain speed with a prop. Then came jet engines, and the speed of airplanes doubled overnight and eventually tripled."[2] Tom Carroll, executive director of the National Commission on Teaching and America's Future, has noted the apocryphal tale of the man who greeted the Wright Brothers after their first successful flight. Unimpressed, the man asked, "Well, that's all well and good, but how will this help us fix the railroads?" The man could understand this revolutionary advance only in terms of its impact on the familiar. Similarly, we routinely look at new learning tools and ask only how they might be used to improve traditional classrooms rather than how they might revolutionize schooling.

Studies have consistently found that classroom technology has not made much difference for student learning or classroom instruction.[3] Perhaps, however, technology is not a way to augment yesterday's classrooms but rather a tool with which to rethink the learning environment. After all, apropos of Carroll's tale, when diesel replaced steam power for the locomotive industry, it significantly reduced the number of service stations and railroad workers needed to monitor diesel-powered engines. Steam required two operating personnel: an engineer to control the throttle and brake and a fireman to keep the fire burning. With diesel locomotives, fuel, water, and air flow could be monitored by a single engineer. The problem was that the firemen weren't about to stand for workforce reductions. Taking advantage of diesel power meant changing labor agreements, not just machinery.[4] Transformation requires not just technological advances but the ability to employ them in smart and cost-effective ways.

Examples of our limited ability to anticipate or gauge the utility of new inventions are legion. In 1861, German inventor Philip Reis created a primitive version of the telephone, but he gave up when no one expressed interest and he could not conceive of a viable commercial application. Fifteen years later, American inventor Alexander Graham Bell had more luck with that. In 1967, MIT graduate Ray Tomlinson began work on developing the ARPAnet, an electronic system designed to maintain military communication in case of a nuclear attack. Along the way, he developed a system for sending messages between multiple computers, and in 1971, he sent the first-ever electronic message between two machines—the first "e-mail." Tomlinson recalls a colleague, Jerry Burchfiel, saying, "Don't tell anyone! This isn't what we're supposed to be working on." When asked what prompted him to send his message, Tomlinson replied, "Mostly because it seemed like a neat idea."[5]

If it is tough to anticipate which inventions will prove useful, it may be even harder to predict which ventures will succeed. Just ask anyone who failed to predict, in 1998, that eBay and Amazon would become remarkably successful or who thought, in the summer of 2007, that household names like Bear Stearns and Washington Mutual were safe bets for a 401(k).

Explaining that its staff had identified 52 design flaws in the game, Parker Brothers twice rejected overtures to buy the rights to Monopoly before finally purchasing the game in 1935. Within its first year, Monopoly became the best-selling board game in America. When the noted English essayist Kenneth

Grahame submitted his manuscript for *The Wind in the Willows* to Charles Scribner, Scribner rejected it, characterizing the volume as "altogether lacking in human interest." Dr. Seuss's first children's book, *And to Think That I Saw It on Mulberry Street*, was rejected by more than 25 publishers before finally being accepted by Vanguard Press. Today, his books have sold more than 500 million copies worldwide.[6] Another volume that numerous publishing houses passed on was *Harry Potter and the Sorcerer's Stone*, the first book in a children's series that has enjoyed some small success.

The Edsel may be the most famous commercial flop of the 20th century. When it was unveiled by the Ford Motor Company in 1958, the Edsel was the most carefully designed car in American automotive history. Its massive failure prompted Ford to rethink its assumptions and market segmentation. The unforeseen result was the Ford Mustang—one of the most *successful* cars in history. Ford hoped to sell 100,000 Mustangs in the model's first year; instead, it sold 1 million.[7]

Robert Laughlin, a 1998 recipient of the Nobel Prize for physics, has admonished, "The search for new things always looks like a lost cause until one makes a discovery. If it were obvious what was there, one would not have to look for it."[8] It should come as no surprise that the challenge of anticipating what will work is magnified when it comes to the turbulent, sprawling, complex realms of schooling. Finding successful solutions in schooling is indeed different from doing so in areas like automobiles or publishing, but the key lesson is that expertise, resources, and research do not guarantee foresight or success—in any field.

While entrepreneurship is uncertain, however, it is not haphazard. Matt Candler, whom we met in Chapter 1, offers a good illustration. In his first year in charge of new school development at KIPP, the organization got a "green light" for a dramatic expansion—opening schools in 10 new cities. Sites were required to have facilities, operational flexibility, and solid leaders in place in order to move forward, and Candler monitored the progress of each startup using a management system he learned when working on the Atlanta Committee for the 1996 Olympic Games. Candler explains, "For each [sports] venue that we managed, we listed the tasks that had to be completed and by when. We then built a giant map of miniature timelines—one for each task—that provided an easy way to see the whole project and discuss dependencies between tasks. There were 406 items on our 2002 Gantt charter template. . . . We handed each [charter school] founder a four-foot-long 'Gantt chart' rolled up in scroll fashion with a bow tied around it. This was partly to scare them about how hard starting a school was and partly to assure them that we had a handle on what it took."[9] Smart entrepreneurs do what they can to stack the odds in their favor.

Getting Past "More, Better"

A greenfield approach is not about "more, better" solutions to today's problems. It requires not that every entrepreneur devise a better schoolhouse—a new, miracle lab school—but a solution that can solve one substantial problem for students, teachers, or schools. No one suggested that Amazon should be taken seriously only if it opened a chain of brick-and-mortar stores a la Barnes & Noble and sought to do everything Barnes & Noble already did but better. Yet, in K–12 schooling, devising a great niche service is not enough; the constant expectation is that entrepreneurs should seek to do everything and launch a new "whole school" model.

There is a fascination among public officials and philanthropists with high-powered charter schools in urban communities. This enthusiasm is natural enough, as schools like Achievement First and YES Prep are posting impressive results while serving at-risk kids. However, observers often don't realize that these schools generally succeed by hiring smart people, extending the school day, and creating disciplined cultures—in the words of author David Whitman, by embracing their paternalistic role and "sweating the small stuff."[10] These schools do what good schools have always aspired to do, but do more of it and do it better. This "more, better" approach emphasizes conventional, expensive means, such as increasing instructional time, and a tendency to favor reformers who *augment* rather than *reinvent* familiar school models. But it also tilts the playing field against providers who are pioneering wholly new and perhaps *dramatically* better ways of addressing challenges that may not adhere to the "whole school" model.

The "whole school" expectation also makes it harder to specialize and requires entrepreneurs to do things that they may not be good at. Even if their expertise is in designing curricula for middle school math or helping English language learners master English, entrepreneurs find themselves struggling to launch new schools and tackling everything from facilities to information systems.

A persistent challenge, not unique to education, is that even policymakers and reformers heralded for their entrepreneurial bent are typically more enamored of yesterday's entrepreneurial successes than they are interested in nurturing tomorrow's. More than a few cutting-edge superintendents have addressed school reinvention by identifying some successful models and saying, "I want more of those." This can impede the search for new, better solutions.

Chris Whittle, who founded Edison Schools back in 1992, has noted, "I've often said that Edison's schools are the 'best of the old world' in schools. We've successfully brought together, under one school roof, many of the best design elements out there. . . . But we have yet to bring about our most important innovation: a school design that provides a highly unusual student and teacher experience and radically superior results."[11]

Similarly, the KIPP Academies have an impressive track record and national recognition, but those responsible are the first to acknowledge that their greatest triumph is proficiently executing a traditional model of schooling. As Mike Feinberg, cofounder of the KIPP Academies, has noted, "There's no secret sauce to KIPP. It's great teaching and more of it."[12] KIPP has succeeded primarily by focusing on results, recruiting talented teachers and school leaders, and forging a culture of commitment and hard work. KIPP and its kin deserve the admiration and accolades they receive, but they should be regarded as the early fruits of greenfield endeavors and not the end of the line.

Now, some observers suggest that Feinberg's recipe reflects excessive modesty. For instance, Steven Wilson, founder of Ascend Learning and author of *Learning on the Job*, has suggested that KIPP's changes to staffing and management are more radical than Feinberg's self-deprecating demurral might suggest—and that these innovations are crucial to KIPP's success. To the degree that this is true, to the extent that high-performing school builders are successful because they are pioneering smarter approaches to management or staffing, it is critical that the full scope of the innovation be understood and expansion efforts be pursued with careful attention to the entire model and not just to its most visible components. Otherwise, we risk misinterpreting or misapplying lessons.

Ultimately, school builders are just one element of a vibrant ecosystem. Specialized new providers can help erect and finance facilities, recruit and train educators and school leaders, use technology to deliver or enhance instruction, offer data systems and management, craft curricula and instructional materials, and provide high-quality assessment and performance analysis. In doing so, they can ease the burdens on teachers and schools and increase the likelihood of dramatic, replicable advances in teaching and learning.

Consider the persistent problem of boosting college attendance among low-income students. Less than 50 percent of low-income high school graduates enroll in college. However, Washington, DC–based College Summit, founded in 1993 by J. B. Schramm, has significantly increased college-going rates in partner schools while serving more than 10,000 students a year. Its methods include attention to mentoring, peer influence, a structured curriculum, and the use of online tools to help teachers and students manage the application process. Devoting particular attention to those students whose choices influence those of their peers, College Summit has helped send 79 percent of the 9,500 low-income "student influencers" it has mentored to college—and 80 percent of them have graduated.[13] College Summit's approach features an intense commitment to data. The organization's staff provides partner schools with monthly data on key indicators—such as percentage of a senior class making lists of colleges they are interested in applying to, completing the personal statements required for applications, and going on to submit applications—that are essential to transitioning students to college. Its specific mission and ability to operate in multiple locales has allowed College Summit to acquire expertise and focus its energies in a way that most schools and districts cannot.

State and district leaders can make it easier for accountable leaders to tap into effective service providers like College Summit by promoting flexibility in budgeting and staffing. They can encourage those same leaders to aggressively seek out effective providers by promoting a strong performance culture.

Greenfield Is Not "School Choice"

Skeptics of a best practice approach and other conventional reform strategies have most frequently turned to "choice-based" reform—such as school vouchers or charter schooling—which are intended to allow families to seek better schools and subject districts to competition. However, if best practices trust too readily in our ability to improve outdated institutions, choice-based reform trusts too readily in the notion that allowing families to choose schools will transform K–12 education or dramatically boost school quality.

A common mistake is to conflate greenfield schooling with choice-based reform. Now, let's be clear: Other things being equal, strong charter schooling and school voucher programs are good and powerful ways to clear the path for greenfield school builders. Ultimately, however, greenfield is not about choices but about dynamic problem solving and Joseph Schumpeter's call for "creative destruction."

Greenfield requires that choice be coupled with opportunities for entrepreneurs to enter the field, obtain resources, recruit talent, try new approaches, develop new products, compete fairly, and benefit from their successes. School choice helps create the condition for greenfield and foster entrepreneurship only to the extent that it promotes these opportunities.

Ensuring that parental choice helps to create greenfield also requires that money actually flows to good ideas, families have good information when making choices, successful providers are rewarded and encouraged to grow, and failure brings real consequences. Today, those conditions too rarely hold.

Proposals for charter schooling or school vouchers have paid little attention to the development of the infrastructure, quality control, and policy environment needed to turn school choice plans into greenfield. Choice plans have routinely skipped past the lack of human and venture capital that characterizes other dynamic sectors, or the reality that offering parents a choice of institution does little or nothing to foster new opportunities for more specialized tool builders or talent hunters. This state of affairs helps to explain the uneven record of choice programs to date.

In fact, as we will note in Chapter 3, many tool builders seeking to supply schools with better data systems, instructional tools, or technology actually find that school choice can be an impediment, as fragmentation in the market makes it even more difficult to build a sustainable business. Creating greenfield, then, is anything but a simple question of school choice. Allowing all parents more opportunity to select a school is but one small step in the process of creating room for dynamic problem solvers, whether inside or outside of traditional systems.

Creating Greenfield Conditions

Some environments are more hospitable to entrepreneurs than others. A crucial starting point is creating room for new ventures to take root, and, as noted, school choice and charter schooling can be vital ways to do this. As Dacia Toll, president of Achievement First, says, "Charter schooling was essential for our success. It gave us a blank slate with total control over our budget, over hiring, and our program." But such opportunities provide only a start. The biotechnology or software industries are flush with funding and enjoy dense networks of entrepreneurial talent; education, in comparison, is a barren garden where few new seedlings thrive. Cultivating these ventures requires not just giving them legal permission to operate but also providing the metaphorical chicken wire, fertilizer, and bamboo stakes that can help tender saplings take firm root and flourish.

In education, high-quality ventures are more likely to emerge and thrive when the rules are stable, when there is a body of knowledge and research to leverage, when performance can be measured in smart and accurate ways, and when new ventures are able to tap into resources, expertise, and talent. Vibrant markets depend on transparency, predictability, human talent, financial resources, and opportunities. Nobel laureate Milton Friedman observed, "In some ways, referring to 'the market' puts the discussion on the wrong basis. The market is not a cow to be milked; neither is it a sure-fire cure for all ills."[14] As the dot-com bubble, the housing bubble, and the banking crisis have reminded us in recent years, markets can yield horrific results if they are ill-constructed or marked by perverse incentives.

Efforts to foster greenfield in other sectors can inform our thinking in schooling. Recall the disheartening experience in 2003 that followed American success in toppling Saddam Hussein in Iraq. Overly optimistic observers imagined that the vacuum created by the dictator's fall would be filled by democratic practices and economic revival as Iraqis reveled in their new freedom. Instead, disorder ensued, and it took several years until a sustained effort to address the violence, create viable institutions, and seed new businesses finally started to provide the foundations for a stable society. Whether the subject is refashioning an entire government or a single sector, creating a vacuum is no panacea; what matters is what fills the void.

China's heralded, gradual introduction of a market economy within a single-party, communist state illustrates how a vibrant supply side can emerge even under seemingly prohibitive conditions—and offers a useful example for nurturing entrepreneurial activity in U.S. education. Over the past three decades, China's totalitarian regime has enjoyed enormous success liberalizing its economy and fostering growth, even as it has maintained repressive political and social policies. It has done so by cultivating human capital, encouraging foreign direct investment, fostering a more responsive banking system, and boosting investment in research and development. China's communist rulers streamlined the state workforce, shuttered tens of thousands of inefficient state-owned enterprises, and restructured or dismantled stagnant monopolies.[15] China's transition featured careful attention to market design, with World

Bank economist Shahid Javed Burki observing that the Chinese government "created space for economic innovation while minimizing the political risks that make the Chinese reticent to embrace far-reaching or dramatic reforms."[16]

In the United States, efforts to deregulate domestic airlines in the 1970s illustrate the complexities of cultivating a dynamic marketplace in the wake of bureaucracy and regulation. Major airports could handle only so many takeoffs and landings per hour, and exclusive gate leases previously granted to airlines stifled competitors and limited the number of available flights. Newer carriers paid higher prices and were restricted to off-peak times. As economists Steven Morrison and Clifford Winston noted, "New entrants are not prevented from serving these airports. New entrants are, however, prevented from serving airports if they cannot get takeoff and landing slots or gates."[17] Furthermore, regulations and contracts also limited the ability of existing airlines to adjust the size of flight crews, to assign personnel based on performance rather than seniority, or to rapidly prepare planes for their next flight. This hobbled the legacy carriers, which were overtaken by new ventures like Southwest and JetBlue.

Nurturing Entrepreneurship

Fostering a supply of quality providers requires creating opportunity and making the money, talent, and infrastructure available to fuel entrepreneurial efforts. Too often, education lacks these basic elements of greenfield. As in Iraq in the years following the fall of Saddam Hussein, there are inadequate efforts to build private entities or spur the investment capital and talent needed for vibrant growth. As in China before the reforms, would-be entrepreneurs are stifled by policies and routines. And as with the airlines in the 1970s, chokepoints impede new entrants and slow the expansion of even successful operators.

If promising ventures are to fulfill their potential, entrepreneurs must be encouraged to serve as many students, educators, and schools as possible. That is not the culture of schooling today. Teachers and schools serve the kids who show up; districts serve the children who live in the community. Period. A similar mind-set pervades in most charter and private schools, as well.

Educators in admired charter schools are often reluctant to try replicating their school's approach elsewhere because—unlike private-sector counterparts, who enjoy professional and monetary benefits from growth—most of the rewards successful charter school educators experience are intrinsic ones.

They enjoy running their schools, working with teachers, and seeing students learn. Spending less time in their school and more time fundraising, hiring staff, and managing multiple locations is unappealing. For this reason, even many talented and highly successful charter school principals express little desire to maximize enrollment or embark on ambitious growth plans. This attitude makes complete sense; if Henry Ford or Bill Gates stood to reap little monetary or professional reward for building giant organizations that could serve millions of customers, they probably would have been happy to tinker in the garage and forgo all the headaches and sleepless nights.

In fact, the web of obstacles and the lack of available support for entrepreneurs might drive would-be entrepreneurs right back into their garage. In 1994, two young Teach For America corps members teaching in the Houston Independent School District (HISD) set out to launch a new program for 5th graders on the second floor of Garcia Elementary. The district had few resources to offer, but the two young men wrote more than 100 letters to potential funders and raised the few thousand dollars they needed for materials and supplies. The program proved successful, and after two years, it outgrew its space. The reward for this success was a district decree that students would have to leave the program to attend their zoned middle schools.

Refusing to acquiesce, the two teachers reached out to the HISD central office. They hit a wall and were unable even to obtain an appointment with the superintendent. One of the two responded by settling in for a long afternoon on the hood of Superintendent Rod Paige's pickup, waiting for him to emerge from the district's downtown offices. Finally, with Paige's help, they overrode district policy and secured space. This is illustrative of the hurdles Mike Feinberg and David Levin had to clear in launching the first KIPP Academy. It's not just that the current education establishment doesn't nurture entrepreneurs; our school districts too often seem inclined to dismiss entrepreneurs as a nuisance.

Indeed, political currents can stifle new efforts, even in the case of potentially meritorious innovations. The nature of K–12 schooling means that many new providers require some kind of state okay to operate. For charter schools, that is a charter school law that sets out the requirements for schools to open. For talent providers, that can be permission from the state department of education or legislature to operate as a state-approved alternative training program. Winning over state officials can exact a toll in terms of both energy and the ability of new providers to bluntly challenge the status quo. I'll have much more to say on these political challenges in Chapter 3.

Finally, systematic investment in new, promising, entrepreneurial efforts is simply not part of American schooling the way it is in other industries. In the U.S. economy, it is estimated that more than a thousand new business ventures are born every hour of every working day.[18] Several thousand U.S. firms receive venture capital funding each year. The National Venture Capital Association reports that in 2005, 182 venture capital funds attracted $25.2 billion in new investment.[19] That is a lot of new ideas and a lot of resources. In the whole of the U.S. economy, 11 percent of jobs involve either starting or managing new businesses. Even in France, hardly a hotbed of entrepreneurship, the ratio is over 5 percent. What is the figure for the education sector? The figure is so small that analysts lump together education and social services, yielding a combined total of zero percent.[20]

Negotiating Perilous Political Terrain

The American Board for Certification of Teacher Excellence (ABCTE) is a nonprofit organization founded in 2001 that seeks to recruit talented career changers into teaching. It offers a rigorous but straightforward set of examinations in content and pedagogical expertise intended to allow qualified applicants to bypass traditional preparation programs. The organization's effort immediately encountered skepticism from state regulatory bodies and strong opposition from colleges of education and teachers unions. This was a particular problem given that, in each state where it operates, ABCTE requires state approval to operate as a recognized alternative route to certification.

In 2005, Dave Saba was recruited from Kaplan Test Preparation to become the president of ABCTE. As he recalls, "The biggest obstacle to our expansion was that we were considered by the education establishment to be a group that wanted to 'blow up' traditional teacher preparation and dominate the teacher-certification market [even though] this was never part of our mission. We were founded as one possible solution to a critical problem: the nation's growing shortage of quality teachers, especially in math and the sciences. State education leaders are more open to embracing new ideas when not attached to an ideology strongly associated with one side of the political spectrum. They want solutions without controversy."

As for the groups that ABCTE had to fight to gain acceptance in new states, Saba says, "We listened closely to those that opposed us so that we could address their objections and ease their skepticism. . . . We eliminated the rhetoric and refined our message so that stakeholders understood the positive impact we could bring to their state." The result, Saba notes, is that "we no longer beg for meetings with state education agencies. We have added five new states and have many more states looking at the program." Reticence can be the price of admission.

The Role of R&D

Research and development (R&D) is critical to the success of entrepreneurial efforts. Breakthroughs leverage new advances in tools, technology, processes, or management approaches, and the pace of those advances determines how fast and far entrepreneurs can go. Unfortunately, R&D in education has been limited. Anthony Bryk, president of the Carnegie Foundation for the Advancement of Teaching, notes that "the whale of technology . . . has changed virtually every workplace except schools." He adds, "In other sectors of society, leaders confronting such challenges would turn to their research and development communities for guidance," but that approach is not feasible in education, where R&D is limited by institutional arrangements.[21]

In medicine and engineering, research spending accounts for about 5 to 15 percent of total expenditures, with about 20 percent of R&D expenditures going toward basic research and about 80 percent toward design and systematic development.[22] In contrast, even though education spending is well over $500 billion a year, less than a billion of that is invested in educational R&D— or less than a quarter of 1 percent of the overall education budget.[23] K–12 spending is almost entirely consumed by expenses on salaries and operations instead of investments in future solutions.

When it comes to divvying up education dollars, R&D is too often an afterthought. Larry Berger and David Stevenson of Wireless Generation point out that the federal government spends 100 times as much on medical research as it does on education research. They cite Marcia Angell's argument in *The Truth About the Drug Companies* that although pharmaceutical and medical device firms "like to present themselves as engines of innovation and discovery, it turns out that the health sciences R&D climate in the United States—and most of the breakthroughs—depend largely on *government* funding of innovation through the NIH [National Institutes of Health] and at universities."[24] While an increased federal role makes greenfielders nervous, there is a crucial place for Uncle Sam to invest in the research and evaluation that fuels entrepreneurship.

When it comes to taking research and turning it into something useful, though, it is commercial providers—not researchers or government officials—

who typically have the requisite incentive, capacity, and tools. In education, commercial providers routinely provide textbooks, curriculum, software, assessments, and professional development. These firms are far from flawless, but they do have incentives to market services to lots of districts and states, to focus on replicable advances, and to promote designs that are easy to share and implement. They also understand the factors that shape purchasing decisions and what state and district approval mechanisms require. Unfortunately, although these for-profit firms are best equipped to *develop* research into something useful, researchers and practitioners are often uncomfortable working with them and thus keep them at arm's length. Meanwhile, these working relationships are commonplace in R&D-intensive sectors like aerospace and biotech.

When commercial investors or firms are not playing the R&D role, it is sometimes essential for philanthropy or nonprofits to step in. In health care, biopharmaceutical companies frequently rely on philanthropic support for the initial stages of new drug testing, which present too much risk to attract venture capital. When such support is lacking, new drugs for rare diseases may go undeveloped due to the sizable expense involved and limited potential payoff.[25] Funders strive to provide support to bridge this chasm so that promising research does not languish in the lab.

Entrepreneurship is about devising new and improved solutions to our challenges. R&D generates the raw material that fuels those solutions: knowledge, whether in the form of new tools, technology, or organizational strategies. R&D requires patience that we too often lack in the education arena. Medical and technological breakthroughs today are often seeded by expensive investments made 10 or 20 years ago, or even longer. The payoff for boosting K–12 R&D will not be wondrous increases in student achievement in three months or three years; it will unfold only in the course of time. This is a difficult sale in the "fix it now" world of schooling, but creating greenfield is a task that demands patience.

The Role of For-Profits

When it comes to educational entrepreneurship, nonprofits enjoy visible successes and glowing press coverage while avoiding the unpleasant question of self-interest that plagues profit-seeking ventures. Especially in schooling, where questions of the public good loom large, nonprofits that marry idealistic passion and entrepreneurial energy are a welcome force. By virtue of being nonprofit, these organizations face fewer obstacles under state charter school laws, find it easier to pursue philanthropic support, and are less likely to encounter organized political opposition.

That said, it is important to appreciate the unique strengths of for-profit enterprises. Today, for-profit firms constitute about $25 billion of the $600 billion K–12 sector, with most of this money earned by giant publishing and testing firms and the rest by smaller providers in areas like technology, professional development, and school improvement.[26]

When weighing the role of for-profits, there are several things worth keeping in mind. First, because for-profits seek to earn competitive returns for investors, promising entrepreneurs are positioned to tap vast sums through private equity markets. Second, for-profits are driven by a relentless imperative to seek out and adopt cost efficiencies, where nonprofit managers will typically have less incentive to cut expenses. Third, for-profits have self-interested and professional cause to expand more rapidly than nonprofits. Fourth, for-profits are focused on a bottom line and are therefore more willing to reduce output or withdraw from an industry when circumstances warrant, allowing them to correct course or reallocate resources more rapidly. In short, for-profit organizations can be more nimble and quick-footed. Finally, scholars have noted that for-profits typically fare better than nonprofits at attracting managerial and technical talent because they can provide more rewards for performance and opportunities for professional growth.[27]

Nonprofits have little incentive to become "early adopters" of cheaper or more uncertain tools and techniques. For example, if substituting online training for in-person professional development is shown to be as effective and cheaper, it would seem to make sense for managers to adopt it. The reality is that managers may have longstanding relationships with trainers, veteran employees may enjoy workshop travel or distrust online training, and parents of schoolchildren may perceive online professional development as a second-rate alternative to "the real thing." Risk taking is an issue for both for-profits and nonprofits, but without investors pushing aggressively for new efficiencies or cost savings, nonprofits tend to move much more slowly. There is an obvious downside associated with for-profit providers embracing new tools and technologies too quickly or thoughtlessly, but this merely underscores the need for both a healthy diversity of providers and smart accountability.

The private sector's uneven record reminds us that for-profits have their own significant limitations, to say the least. The incentive to cut costs can lead businesses to cut corners. The urge to grow can lead to unacceptable compromises in quality. These are real concerns that require educational leaders to take a careful look at the performance and cost-effectiveness of competing vendors. Of course, as more than one entrepreneur-friendly superintendent has said with exasperation, "That's part of the job description!" Whatever legitimate concerns exist about for-profits, none of them should be taken to suggest that nonprofits can readily match for-profit firms' dexterity, capacity for scale, and inclination toward aggressive cost cutting. When it comes to rethinking teaching and learning, there are vital roles for both nonprofits and for-profits.

Cultivating Greenfield

The promise of greenfield schooling rests on the emergence of dynamic, growth-oriented problem solvers. Whether these problem solvers proliferate or thrive depends critically on the environment in which they take root. The task for greenfield reformers is to create supportive, dynamic environments. In doing so, four tasks are crucial: removing obstacles, ensuring quality, and supplying both talent and financial resources. Those elements, in turn, are the subjects of the next four chapters. Before we proceed, though, a brief overview is in order.

Schooling is suffused with *barriers* that hinder would-be entrepreneurs. These obstacles take two main forms: formal barriers, such as laws and regulations, and informal impediments, which are less visible and more subtle. The first category includes regulations that might hamper the opening of a charter school, state licensure systems that can make it costly and onerous for candidates to obtain alternative teaching certification, and textbook approval systems so arduous that only the largest publishers are able to compete. The second category includes political sniping, operational routines, and cultural norms.

Second, greenfield creates opportunities for great providers and ultimately serves kids well only if *quality* is pervasive—if performance is transparent and if formal and informal mechanisms are flagging both stellar providers and inept ones. States and districts have long maintained bureaucratic reporting systems focused on tracking *inputs* like attendance, teacher credentials, and expenditures while paying insufficient attention to *outputs*. Difficulty in gauging whether new ventures are good or cost-effective stifles entrepreneurs and yields a focus on bureaucratic process rather than whether kids are learning. Only in the past decade have metrics progressed much beyond spending and enrollment to measure how much students are learning—at least in the core subjects of reading and math. Yet, even today, the existing output metrics and quality-control efforts only scratch the surface of what a greenfield sector requires.

Third, an entrepreneurial environment relies on *human capital*: entrepreneurs ready to seize new opportunities and talented professionals available to staff new ventures. In vibrant sectors, this pipeline is rich and deep and is coupled with an array of providers, investors, and personal networks spanning academe, industry, and finance. Yet, in schooling, there is a dearth of individuals inclined or prepared to thrive in this capacity. Moreover, young teachers generally work alone in their classrooms, have few school-related responsibilities outside their own classrooms, and develop professional networks restricted to fellow teachers. As a result, a teacher's circle of contacts is often limited to his or her peers and provides little opportunity for the kind of professional development more likely to nurture entrepreneurial leaders. Successful new enterprises like the NewSchools Venture Fund, New Schools for New Orleans, The Broad Foundation, and Education Pioneers are developing programs and networks that are gradually changing this situation, but it will take much more in the way of creative thinking, talent development, and infrastructure to provide entrepreneurial efforts with the human capital they need to produce a lasting impact on the education sector.

Finally, the availability of *financial capital* to support promising ventures is crucial to their long-term viability. In education, little private capital is directed to startups; there is almost no infrastructure to help interested investors and entrepreneurs locate one another; and there is no network of existing entrepreneurs and venture capitalists that serves to surface and nurture new enterprises. Meanwhile, the public dollars that make up more than 90 percent of K–12 spending rarely support entrepreneurial problem solving. This means that philanthropic giving, although it amounts to a fraction of 1 percent of total education spending, has played an outsized role in the launch of greenfield ventures. In the private sector, the torrent of venture capital is accompanied by an ecosystem of institutions and actors. In education, especially when it comes to directing public and philanthropic dollars, such infrastructure is missing. Meanwhile, the venture capital communities that have sprung up in technology corridors like Silicon Valley and Route 128 in Boston are not plugged into the education world. The trick is to better understand what it will take for education dollars to drive transformation.

Let's start by considering the question of barriers.

3

BARRIERS

WHEN CULTIVATING LAND, the first step is to clear away the rubble that can choke off growth. The same is true when it comes to preparing greenfield. It begins by knocking down obstacles—both those that are formal and visible and those that are more subtle and easier to overlook—to permit the emergence and growth of problem-solving ventures.

Formal barriers are laws or rules that make it difficult or impossible to launch and expand new ventures. These include statutes that prohibit or limit the number of charter schools, restrict alternative licensure of teachers and administrators, or require lengthy and extensive textbook-approval processes that only industry giants can navigate or afford. Informal barriers are the political, operational, and cultural routines that make it difficult for new ventures to gain a foothold or pioneer new practices. Most ventures face both kinds of obstacles. The extent and variety of barriers force entrepreneurs to compromise their models and slow their efforts to win allies and appease enemies.

Because successful entrepreneurial efforts become brand names while unsuccessful ones fade away, we can forget how difficult launching a new venture is even for providers that have come to be widely admired. Teach For America almost died on the vine in the mid-1990s due to political hostility and nervous funders. The KIPP Academies, as we noted in the last chapter, might never have gotten started. New York City–based New Leaders for New Schools (NLNS) is a principal-recruitment and -training venture that today operates in nearly a dozen cities and is awash in recognition and support. Yet,

44

as a young organization, NLNS struggled mightily just to convince districts to hire its graduates. As journalist Alexander Russo reported at the time,

> Finding accomplished aspirants has not [been a challenge]. In 2003 the program received more than 1,000 completed applications for just 55 spots. . . . Despite their accomplishments and passion, [however], New Leaders fellows have had a hard time breaking into traditional public schools, especially those fellows who lack contacts or extensive experience in education. It's not that New Leaders can't get work; nearly all of the New Leaders have secured education-related jobs. But just 5 of the first 15 graduates and just over half of the 32 graduates in 2003 found positions running schools of any type.[1]

Many of today's barriers are not the result of conscious design but the consequence of policies, rules, and practices that have accreted over time. They may have once been innocuous but now represent a drag on creative problem solving. Procurement practices insensitive to cost-effectiveness or budgeting rules that make it tough for districts to reconfigure staffing create barriers that may owe more to inertia than anything else.

Successful K–12 entrepreneurs constitute just a tiny sliver of the system, often surviving at the whim of an entrepreneur-friendly superintendent or governor. When that individual leaves, all bets can be off. Greenfield schooling begins by reducing barriers so that entrepreneurs are less dependent on a handful of friendly environs.

The Impact of Formal Barriers

Understanding the source of the formal barriers, like statutes, rules, and contracts, begins with a simple insight into the general nature of government agencies. As Stanford University political scientist Terry Moe has explained, public policies, regulations, and the bureaucratic agencies that implement them are inevitably influenced, and frequently dominated, by active interest groups.[2] These interest groups wield influence in legislatures and at every level of the rule-making and implementation process. Those seeking to fundamentally alter established routines in a publicly controlled sector like education must take on the unions, major textbook companies, teachers colleges, and associations of school boards and school administrators that support them.

These barriers are common to school builders, tool builders, and human capital providers, but there are also distinctive obstacles that confront each of these groups. Entrepreneur-friendly charter school laws provide equitable funding, help with facilities and financing, minimize intrusive rules on staffing or management, and do not place caps on the number of charter schools. Greenfield laws governing human capital providers streamline requirements for prospective teachers, create new entry points through nontraditional recruiting and training programs, and make it easy for districts or charter schools to partner with talent providers. Greenfield for tool builders eliminates legal requirements that make it hard for new providers to compete and minimizes tortuous procurement rules that stymie ventures that lack a personal contact or a huge sales force.

School Builders

Charter schooling is predicated on the idea of freeing entrepreneurial public schools from many or most bureaucratic rules and regulations in exchange for being held accountable for specified performance targets. Minnesota enacted the first charter school law in 1991; today, more than 4,600 charter schools enroll more than 1.4 million students in 40 states.[3] More than 350,000 students are on waiting lists for charter schools.[4]

The growth of alternative public schools has been constrained by state policies that cap the number of charters that can be issued, limit funding, or impose heavy-handed regulations. Twenty-six states have some form of legislative cap on the total number of charter schools that may operate.[5] Other states, such as Indiana and New Hampshire, limit the number of charters that can be issued each year.

State policies also constrain the number and type of charter schools by tightly restricting the organizations authorized to issue charters. In 2007, the U.S. Department of Education reported that nearly 90 percent of the nation's more than 800 charter school authorizers are the local school districts themselves.[6] Placing the local school district in charge of authorizing charters is problematic because districts are often reluctant to expand the number of alternatives to their own traditional schools. A couple of years ago, the school board of Calvert County, Maryland, denied a charter for "many major and minor deficiencies" only to have the Maryland State Board of Education read the same application and deem it "thorough and well-developed."[7] When the state board asked the county board to renegotiate, it refused. Such tales are common. While local districts represent 90 percent of all authorizers, they authorize fewer than half of charter schools, and 8 out of 10 districts have authorized just one or two charters.[8]

State laws that enable charter creation are necessary, but they are insufficient for promoting greenfield for school builders. Smart quality control and operational flexibility are critical, as are sensible state policies on charter financing, regulation, and accountability. Most states provide significantly less funding to charters than to district schools. The Thomas B. Fordham Institute has reported that "the finance ground rules appear designed to produce failure, not success, on the part of charter schools."[9] This study of 17 states during the 2002–03 school year found that some states treated charter schools much more equitably than others, with the per-pupil funding disparity between charter and district schools ranging from a 5 percent disadvantage for charters in New Mexico to a 40 percent disadvantage in South Carolina.[10] Similarly, the Center for Education Reform (CER) studied 40 states in 2005 and estimated that per-pupil charter school funding was, on average, 21 percent below that for traditional district schools.[11] CER reported that the reasons charter schools receive less funding include the inequitable allocation of grants from local, state, and federal governments; "hold harmless" clauses that prevent funds from following students when they transfer to charter schools; local districts simply withholding funds for charters; and the fact that many states provide facilities support to district schools but not to charters. Inadequate support both deters prospective charter entrepreneurs and handicaps existing charter schools.

Charter schools also benefit when granted autonomy over hiring, budgets, curricula, and scheduling, which frees them to explore new and potentially more effective approaches. Greenfield requires the creation of what Drew University political scientist Patrick McGuinn has termed "entrepreneurial space"[12]—freedom from onerous regulation of operations. Though predicated on increased autonomy, charters have been granted less freedom than some might imagine. According to the Education Commission of the States, all state charter laws provide some kind of waiver from state regulations, but just 6 states automatically waive state and district laws and regulations and another 16 states automatically waive some number of specified provisions. In the other half of charter states, each charter school must petition for specific waivers.[13] A 2004 U.S. Department of Education report noted that 35 to 45 percent of charter schools reported having limited authority over curriculum, school calendar, assessment, and discipline.[14] This report also revealed that when it comes to the essential ability to staff their schools, many charters are limited by district collective bargaining agreements, and a quarter have limited authority over hiring and firing.[15] The No Child Left Behind act's "highly qualified teacher" provision has subjected charters to a variety of state-determined rules governing teacher credentialing and licensure.

The language of state charter laws can have unintended consequences. Consider the significant barrier to entry represented by laws that prohibit charter schools from being "home-based." These prohibitions sprang from legislators seeking to prevent homeschoolers from claiming charter school status and receiving public funds. With the advent of Web-based and virtual learning, however, these provisions effectively deny funding to virtual public school models in which children work remotely with a teacher.

Virtual school advocates and entrepreneurs have been required to navigate thorny legislative turf. South Carolina provides a useful illustration of how this works. Encouraged by supportive state education leaders to bring its virtual school model to the state, virtual schooling and curriculum provider K12 Inc. began working in 2004 to have legislators remove the home-based prohibition. Charles Zogby, senior vice president of education and policy at K12, explains, "Lawmakers agreed in 2006 to clarify [that] charter schools could offer virtual services, but required further state law and regulation before virtual learning could be delivered. Even before the ink was dry, we were back at work with legislative leaders to draft a virtual school bill. . . . Several hearings, many meetings, and countless discussions later, a version of the virtual school bill became law in the spring of 2007." The first virtual schools opened in South Carolina in 2008.

The Obstacles to School Building

Ben Cope is development director for the TEAM Charter Schools in Newark, New Jersey. A regional KIPP network, TEAM operates three middle and high schools serving more than 1,000 urban students and aims to grow rapidly to serve 5 percent of Newark's students by 2015 without compromising quality.

Cope notes that this is a daunting goal: "From the beginning of our growth, we have held educational quality paramount, ensuring that we have three critical criteria addressed before moving forward with opening new schools." Cope explains that the first two critical "gates" are finding excellent school leaders and exceptional teachers, and that the pool of available teachers and leaders that meet the TEAM's criteria is limited, due in part to competition "from other charters and education reform efforts within traditional public schools." TEAM's response is to boost recruiting, build a fellows program for new teachers, and look to partner with schools of education and innovative preparation programs like Hunter College's Teacher U to secure new talent.

Beyond that, notes Cope, "the third major challenge to opening new schools is identifying and paying for suitable facilities. Although hiring high-quality educators is a far higher priority than finding the perfect facility, even finding a workable facility for a new school has proved the more difficult challenge in some respects. We have been fortunate to get the city's support in providing shared public school space during the first two years of our high school's operations, but shared space in Newark has, so far, only provided a temporary solution and one that can come with a host of logistical challenges."

Moreover, he explains, "In New Jersey, unlike New York City and Washington, DC, there is no funding provided to charter schools for facilities. Purchasing and renovating suitable space or building from the ground up" for a new school can "easily run into the tens of millions of dollars. This cost poses a nearly insurmountable challenge, because many major charter funders prefer to support operations" and won't finance capital projects that cost this much. Especially in Newark, where many buildings have a history of industrial production, it is difficult for TEAM to find suitable space for renovation. Currently, TEAM is seeking to work with an investor to buy, renovate, and lease one site and to work with the local archdiocese to potentially lease another site. Cope notes, "These solutions may provide short-term answers to the facility challenge, but do not resolve the long-term challenge of finding and paying for quality facilities."

Talent Providers

Human capital providers occupy an awkward position between tool builders and school builders. Talent providers prefer to deal with organizations that have a predictable need for large numbers of teachers or leaders. While charter schools, private schools, or other schools with heightened autonomy have increased leeway to hire, their personnel needs are also less predictable and less stable than those of larger, traditional districts. At the same time, the various procedural and contractual processes of traditional school systems—including veteran teachers' substantial leeway to transfer to schools of their choice and balky human resources systems whose employees may resent outside partners—mean that districts are often less receptive environments for human capital providers.

State laws govern teacher and administrator licensure, and schools of education hold sway over preparation, presenting human capital providers with stark challenges. State licensure systems routinely dictate that alternative providers of teacher training must partner with the traditional programs that are empowered to license teachers. This often means that entrepreneurial programs must incorporate faculty and instructional time from these partner institutions, whether or not they deem it an optimal use of student time. These partnership requirements raise the cost of these programs and can compromise the quality of greenfield models.

States and districts restrict entry into teaching and school administration via licensure requirements, obligating prospective teachers to complete some form of state-approved teacher preparation. These regulations, along with practices governing compensation and hiring, restrict the entry of new candidates and limit entrepreneurial talent providers.

In the 1980s, several states started to develop alternative certification processes to enable prospective teachers to bypass traditional education school programs. The National Center for Education Information reports that in 2007, all 50 states and the District of Columbia had alternative teacher certification programs in place, with a total of 130 different routes provided by 485 programs. The oldest and most prolific alternative programs are those in California, New Jersey, and Texas, which together have long produced nearly half of the national total of alternatively certified teachers.[16]

Alternative programs for teacher and administrator licensure have given rise to some of the best-known examples of educational entrepreneurship. One such effort is Teach For America, founded in 1989 by Wendy Kopp to recruit and prepare bright college graduates for two years of teaching in high-need classrooms. Alternative credentialing enabled Teach For America to develop innovative processes to prepare teachers, including stringent criteria for candidate selection and a dramatically shortened, six-week preparation experience. TFA has yielded teachers who produce student achievement no worse than those of other teachers who have completed much more costly, yearlong traditional programs.[17]

There is reason to wonder, however, how fully "alternative" licensure has actually lowered the barriers for greenfield providers. A 2007 study published by the Thomas B. Fordham Institute and the National Council on Teacher

Quality (NCTQ) reported, "Most alternate route programs have become mirror images of traditional programs."[18] Based on its analysis, NCTQ has judged, "Despite the promise of new alternate routes to teacher certification for talented liberal arts graduates and mid-career professionals, only six states offer genuine alternate routes."[19] Art Wise, former president of the National Council for the Accreditation of Teacher Education, the professional accrediting organization for schools and departments of education, boasted a few years ago that more than two-thirds of "alternative" programs were being operated by traditional education schools.[20] The experience of Teach For America in Connecticut is a case in point. Although TFA is a state-approved alternate route program, the state has also decreed that all TFA candidates must meet all certification requirements for a teaching license before they begin teaching. In practice, this means the program is "alternative" in name only, making TFA's efforts increasingly untenable. It's a situation that has forced TFA to wade into legislative deliberations—and to consider withdrawing from the state of Connecticut if no fix is possible.

In recent years, states have also begun to reconsider how they license, recruit, and train principals and superintendents. Historically, more than 95 percent of principals and 80 percent of superintendents have risen through the ranks, beginning their careers as teachers and then moving on to become assistant principals, then principals, and so on. All but two states (Michigan and Iowa) require that prospective principals and superintendents be licensed in school administration.[21]

RAND Corporation has reported that "formal barriers such as certification requirements and informal barriers such as district hiring practices all but exclude those without teaching experience from consideration for administrative positions."[22] As we'll discuss more fully later in the chapter, nearly all superintendents and principals receive their formal leadership preparation through education school programs that do not equip them to be entrepreneurial leaders.[23]

Some talent providers, such as High Tech High Graduate School of Education in San Diego and Rice University's Education Entrepreneurship Program for principal preparation at the Jones School of Management in Houston, have sidestepped the licensure hurdle by actually becoming recognized providers of preparation. State boards have approved both programs, empowering High

Tech High and the Jones School of Management to serve as official, state-recognized training programs. Such approval can be time-consuming and politically dicey, and it may require compromising some program elements, but it offers a powerful way for talent providers to overcome obstacles imposed by training and licensure systems.

Tool Builders and Service Providers

The measures that create greenfield for school builders do not necessarily do the same for tool builders or service providers. In fact, entrepreneurs devising new instructional or technological tools can find the proliferation of school choice to be a hindrance because marketing new technology tools or data systems and supporting their adoption is feasible only if providers are serving a certain number of schools or students. Trying to work with a scattered handful of small schools rather than with whole districts can lead to costs that quickly become unsustainable. The fragmented K–12 system—with its 15,000 districts and stew of varied standards, accountability and licensure systems, and procurement processes—presents an enormous hurdle to greenfield ventures trying to operate on a national scale.

Inconsistent rules and metrics make it expensive for entrepreneurs to try to compete in multiple markets and lend an edge to the status quo and established mega-firms. As Ron Packard of virtual homeschooling firm K12 Inc. has explained, "The existence of 50 separate sets of state standards creates enormous complexities for what we do."[24] Customization for 50 different markets is an enormous burden, particularly for small organizations. Indeed, entrepreneurs sometimes describe the challenge of expanding across state lines as akin to opening up a brand new business in every state. As a result, many entrepreneurs have chosen to focus their efforts in one locale; those who have not struggle to maintain focus and consistency while customizing their work appropriately.

One powerful illustration of how federal, state, and district policies constrain tool builders is the experience of tutors operating under the "supplemental educational services" provision of No Child Left Behind. NCLB requires Title I schools that have failed to make "adequate yearly progress" for three or more consecutive years to offer students "supplemental education services" (SES)—typically tutoring. The law also stipulates that these services may be provided by private companies or by the districts themselves.

Although SES might seem an obvious opening for entrepreneurial firms, the administration of the SES process was left in the hands of states and districts. States control who can offer services by establishing lists of approved providers; districts are charged with determining student eligibility, informing parents, managing provider access to school sites, and establishing contracts with individual providers. This has created predictable roadblocks.

Journalist Siobhan Gorman has observed that "within this new marketplace, school districts hold enormous power as a result of their dual role as both program administrator and potential provider. Districts also have little incentive to inform parents of the money available to them for tutoring, since districts get to keep any unused funds."[25] In testimony before Congress, Jeffrey Cohen of Catapult Learning noted, "Providers often contend with seemingly unnecessary obstacles, including district opposition to SES, lack of information about implementation plans, and [local education agency] regulation of state-approved programs."[26]

Tool builders thrive in an environment in which states, districts, or other collectives buy in bulk, establish clear and user-friendly procurement systems, and base purchasing decisions on transparent evaluations of cost and performance. Thus, the same fragmentation that is desirable for school builders is frequently an obstacle to tool builders, and the kind of standardized large-scale purchasing that helps tool builders can stifle school builders.

Informal Hurdles

Beyond federal and state laws and formal district practices, there are several kinds of informal barriers that restrict greenfield. These include public skepticism, political pressures, state and district operational routines, and the culture and mind-set of many educators and education leaders. Many of these have a symbiotic relationship with more formal barriers, with informal cultures, routines, and habits of mind deepening and extending their impact. Merely changing laws does not always have the anticipated benefit, because the legacy of entrenched practices and past laws tends to persist. Would-be reformers have too often been content to win measures that relax formal barriers, not recognizing the degree to which their victories are compromised in practice. Successful greenfield reform requires combating informal barriers in conjunction with the more cut-and-dried, visible ones.

Public Opinion

One major constraint on entrepreneurial ventures is the way Americans typi-cally think and talk about schools. For example, the public likes smaller class sizes and is skeptical of school models that employ larger classes, even though small classes consume enormous resources and the research on their value is mixed.[27] Entrepreneurs who proceed from the presumption that any new school model must feature small classes quickly find themselves limited when it comes to rethinking school design or staffing. Author and education man-agement organization veteran Steven Wilson has termed this "the ideology of class size reduction."[28] Although many charter operators and district reformers privately suggest that reducing staffing costs and using teachers in new ways is essential to breakthrough improvement, only a few have accepted larger class sizes, and even fewer have openly acknowledged doing so.

In the private sector, it normally does not matter if the public approves of how companies like Burger King or Old Navy go about their business. Public opinion is more of a concern for organizations like Blue Cross/Blue Shield, which have extensive dealings with public officials or address areas of sensitive public concern. There is no question that public opinion matters enormously in schooling, where the opportunity to open a school or provide services is subject to political determinations, and where parental distaste can ensure the demise of even terrific proposals.

Parents and local leaders also show a preference for nonprofit, "mom and pop" schools independently run by familiar, local educators. This preference has stifled and slowed the expansion of new ventures, especially those seeking to operate more efficiently. John Chubb, former Stanford University profes-sor and now managing director of the EdisonLearning Institute, has argued, "What is most important about the new entrepreneurship is that it brings to the very heart of public education—at least potentially—the twin engines that drive innovation, quality, and value in the private sector: profit and scale. Virtually all of the goods and services that Americans enjoy are produced by for-profit companies. A large percentage of those goods and services owe their various virtues to the large scale organizations that produce them. Public edu-cation is distinctively not-for-profit and small scale."[29]

Due to their relative novelty, greenfield ventures can also suffer due to misinformation and misconceptions that feed public skepticism. In 2006, the annual *Phi Delta Kappan*/Gallup poll on education asked respondents whether charter schools are "public schools," and whether they are free to teach religion, to charge tuition, or to select students based on ability. While state laws define charters as *public* schools and do indeed prohibit them from teaching religion, charging tuition, or cherry-picking students, just 39 percent of respondents thought charters were "public schools," and 50 percent or more said charters were free to teach religion, charge tuition, or select students based on ability.[30] Respondents were not just confused; they were systematically mistaken in a direction sure to bias them against charter schooling, as analyses of public opinion make clear that the public strongly supports schools that it perceives as "public."[31] Given the public's distaste for exclusive practices like charging tuition or selecting students, the persistence of such misinformation, even two decades after the passage of the first charter school laws, poses a significant hurdle.

To date, even would-be reformers have found it more advisable to cater to the public's prejudices than to challenge them. Creating greenfield will require a much clearer and bolder effort to inform and influence public thinking.

Political Pressures

Tellingly, K–12 entrepreneurs have been thwarted by opposition from political constituencies within and around public education, including teachers unions, school administrators, school boards, and civil rights organizations. In 2009, when the names of various educational entrepreneurs, including Wendy Kopp (founder of Teach For America) and Jon Schnur (cofounder of New Leaders for New Schools), were being floated for senior positions in the Obama administration's Department of Education, the president of the American Association of Colleges of Teacher Education issued a fierce denunciation in a widely circulated letter, declaring, "They are unacceptable in these roles. . . . They have evidenced a constant and intense disregard for working with the organized education community. . . . The proposed team, if appointed, would be a grave disappointment for those of us who are hoping to change the education system in the interest of students."

Political opposition takes many forms and plays out in various venues. A few years ago, author and journalist Joe Williams interviewed more than 400 charter school operators across the United States, studied the challenges they face, and documented in detail the political opposition and "bureaucratic sand" hurled in the faces of charter schools. Williams has compared the plight of charter school operators to the game of "Whac-A-Mole," where political opponents wield the mallet and charters scramble to duck repeated blows, and he has noted hostile tactics through which unions and school district officials prevent charters from accessing facilities, delay the processing of funding, and besmirch reputations. This opposition seizes upon laws and regulations, using them as mallets to whack away at new ventures.[32]

Securing school facilities is an enormous challenge for charter schools—and, not so coincidentally, one point where heel-dragging and opposition are especially evident. In Albany, New York, charter opponents tried to use the city's zoning commission to halt charter school growth. When Albany Preparatory Charter School sought one possible facility, both the city and the Board of Zoning Appeals denied the request on grounds that the proposed building was in a location that was not suitable for a school. Ironically, that very building had served for more than 70 years as a school in the Albany public school system. Deeming the decision "arbitrary and capricious," a state supreme court justice ordered the city to reverse the judgment.[33]

In 2000, California citizens voted on Proposition 39 and approved the requirement that unused public school buildings be offered to charter schools before being made available for other uses. Some districts have blatantly ignored the law. Indeed, two charter schools in southeast San Diego—Fanno Academy and KIPP Adelante Academy—resorted to suing the district for "blatant noncompliance" when school officials denied classroom space to charter schools and instead gave it to private schools that could afford to pay higher rent.[34] Some opposition is even more bare-knuckled. In an article published in *Education Next*, Joe Williams cites a *Boston Globe* report that, in Massachusetts, "Children say their public school teachers have pressed them to sign petitions protesting new charters. School committee members have repeatedly called neighbors, imploring them to step down from charter boards. And flyers have circulated, sounding the death of public schools if a charter school opens."[35] When the University of Wisconsin–Milwaukee considered authorizing charter schools for the first time, the local teachers union and top Milwaukee administrators threatened to ban the university's student teachers (potentially preventing them from fulfilling licensure requirements) if the university approved any charters to be managed by the for-profit Edison Schools (now EdisonLearning).[36]

Ed Kirby, a grizzled veteran of the charter sector, has explained how opposition played out when he was a member of the Massachusetts Board of Elementary and Secondary Education team responsible for implementing the state's charter school initiative. At the time, Massachusetts was regarded as a charter school leader, with strong political backing from the governor and legislature. Within a few years, however, the charter authorizer unit transferred from the governor's office to the Massachusetts Department of Education. As Kirby recounts, the move "placed us in an agency dominated by career bureaucrats generally opposed to charter schools and, in many cases, influenced heavily by the very interest groups who were determined to kill our work. It was a bit like sending the hen to live in the fox den and hoping for the best." Meanwhile, hostile interest groups, along with skeptical journalists and researchers, aggressively investigated each of the state's charter schools and the charter office. Kirby explains that responding to these queries "chewed up tens of thousands of hours of time." At one point, the charter schools and the authorizer team were subject to simultaneous, extensive reviews by four distinct public oversight entities: the Office of the State Auditor, the Office of the Inspector General, the U.S. Department of Education's Office of Civil Rights, and the Massachusetts Education Reform Review Commission. Kirby recalls that "good days felt like being under siege and bad days felt like an all-out street fight."[37]

Such political struggles leave once-green fields barren and repel even the most dogged entrepreneurs. Kirby's wry take: "If I had been a motivated school founder anywhere in the country in 1995, I would have hustled to Massachusetts, given the clarity of the state's charter statute and the relative simplicity of its regulatory burden. In 2008, I would look elsewhere."[38]

Marshaling resources and organizing advocacy groups to combat excessive political opposition is an essential element of greenfield. Yet, swept up in broad policy debates, advocates have paid insufficient attention to combating the varied attacks on entrepreneurs or to minimizing the effect of those disruptions.

Operational Routines

In their innocuous daily operations, state and local district officials engage in a variety of behaviors that frustrate and fluster entrepreneurs. Decentralized decision-making authority, tortuous procurement procedures, inflexibility in staffing and budgeting, and the provision of transportation are all examples of inherited practices that can weigh heavily on entrepreneurs.

In terms of day-to-day operational routines, schooling is too often a nightmare scenario for tool builders and talent providers. Larry Berger, CEO of the Brooklyn-based tool builder Wireless Generation, relates that business students are prone to gape when they learn about the decision-making processes in school districts: "It seems that in education, no one is in charge." Berger has a stock, wistful reply: "If only that were the problem. But the situation is much worse: In education, *everyone* is in charge." As Berger and his colleague David Stevenson have explained, marketing products and services to districts requires companies to win over state policymakers who oversee relevant funding, academic consultants who advise districts, key school board members, the district curriculum leadership, the special education department, the office of research and assessment, the chief information officer, the principals, the individual schools' reading coaches, and others.[39]

Berger and Stevensen note that only a few of these individuals have the budgetary authority to say yes, but that most of them have the ability to say no. Not surprisingly, this process often means slogging through procedures, rather than enabling school leaders to focus on the quality or cost-effectiveness of the tool builder's goods or service. In the end, Berger explains, districts often act haphazardly when deciding what to buy. He notes, "In the final days of the fiscal year, schools sometimes find themselves with money that they must 'use or lose.' At this time, the long, involved process goes out the window. . . . One of the most useful things we have learned from our veteran sales people is always to leave a price proposal behind, even when the district does not seem ready for one. If your proposal is in the desk drawer when use-it-or-lose-it time rolls around, you might just get the lucky call."[40]

Another operational barrier is the "pilot problem." When a district does decide to buy a product, it is often conditional on piloting it in a small number of schools or classrooms. This approach has its virtues, but it can also produce prohibitive headaches for entrepreneurs. When districts are not ready to buy at scale, the startup venture often agrees to a pilot program at a low price. This results in expensive onsite handholding to service the customer and ensure that the high-stakes pilot is successful. An even worse scenario occurs when the pilot fails because the startup cannot afford the necessary handholding, which in turn leads teachers to see the program as one more faddish innovation and adopt a "this too shall pass" attitude. Berger notes that "even when the pilot is successful, the same decision-maker who could not pull the trigger at the outset often rewards the successful pilot with an expansion from ten classrooms to fifteen, or with nothing but a congratulations, because that person never really had much budget authority in the first place."[41]

A third crucial but often overlooked operational barrier is the tendency of district leaders to regard staff time and salaries as sunk costs. Consequently, districts typically do not eliminate teaching or staff positions, even if an innovation allows nine employees to accomplish what used to take ten. The result is that school and district leaders have a hard time seeing labor-saving technologies or services as cost-effective. Tim Daly, CEO of The New Teacher Project, a New York–based venture that helps districts recruit faculty and address human resource challenges, routinely encounters this barrier. Too often, he explains,

> A district would tell us that they loved our work, but that we were too expensive. We'd ask what they meant by "too expensive." They'd say that our teachers were $5,000 to $6,000 per head, and that their Human Resources department could recruit teachers for $100 or $150 per head. When we probed, we'd find that this calculation was based solely on two expenses: fees paid to attend job fairs and ads placed in newspapers. It didn't include any of the costs for staff salaries or benefits, or office space used by the recruiters, or technology infrastructure, or placement costs, or mentoring, etc. They just added up the most readily-tallied costs and divided by the number of teachers hired.

A management style that ignores cost efficiencies in staff time and salaries constitutes an enormous obstacle when trying to convince school systems to purchase a product meant to radically improve efficiency or performance. Rather than ask whether a tutoring program would allow a district to reduce the number of paraprofessionals or whether a more sophisticated diagnostic tool might allow talented elementary teachers to accommodate more students, district and state officials seemingly operate from the premise that technology and service providers must "supplement but not supplant" personnel.

Greenfield requires a wholesale alteration of how state and district officials approach and evaluate procurement decisions. This entails making the costs and benefits of staff and services more transparent, rewarding leaders for focusing on cost-effectiveness, and coaching district officials to evaluate alternatives with productivity in mind.[42] It is no small task, to say the least.

Operational concerns can prove equally problematic for school builders. Headaches surrounding student transportation have been a frequent concern for charter school operators. "Transportation is huge," explains Jamie Callendar, a former Ohio legislator. "In the first few years the districts would outright refuse to provide transportation. Now they make it as inconvenient as possible." In Colorado, buses cannot carry students unless inspected by a specially licensed school bus mechanic. Most of the licensed school bus mechanics in the region were, not surprisingly, employed full-time by districts. The K–6 Ross Montessori School in Carbondale, Colorado, paid $25,000 for a turbo-diesel bus that spent most of its first year sitting unused in the school parking lot. When Ross's principal asked the mechanic in the local district to inspect the bus, the school got the bureaucratic cold shoulder. So Ross's principal called a neighboring district. Shortly before the scheduled inspection, Ross was notified that the appointment was canceled: "They said they didn't want to get involved in the politics of our district," the principal recalled.[43]

All of these district routines and bureaucratic mazes sap the time and energy of entrepreneurs—and the kids ultimately pay the price.

Habits of Mind

While formal hurdles impede educators, the socialization, training, and norms that prevail in schooling dramatically aggravate the challenge of introducing and building entrepreneurial ventures. One instructive example comes from California in the 1980s, where the legislature attempted to address concerns about overly intrusive state regulations by allowing districts to apply for waivers if they could demonstrate that existing laws or rules were hampering educational improvement. Columbia University professor Hank Levin recounts, "Relatively few formal requests for waivers were made . . . fewer than 100 were made in the first year [from more than 1,000 districts]." More surprising, notes Levin, was that aside from requests to waive special education provisions, "the vast majority of all requests for waivers were unnecessary." A review by the legal counsel found that nearly all the proposed measures were permissible under existing law and did not require waivers.[44]

Superintendents and boards mistakenly thought rules were more restrictive than they were or, Levin says, they were using laws and regulations "as a scapegoat . . . to justify maintaining existing practices." Former Memphis superintendent Gerry House similarly recalled telling principals that if district regulations and policies were impeding their efforts, they should request waivers. When she started to receive their requests, she found almost all to be unnecessary and that schools could "establish the proposed, new practices under existing district policies."[45]

Similarly, even though collective bargaining agreements frequently permit more latitude than is often understood, most principals and superintendents persistently fail to take steps to sensibly assign personnel, reward expertise, or target professional development. In a 2008 analysis of work rules, teacher compensation, and personnel policies in the nation's 50 largest districts, Coby Loup and I reported that most had substantial opportunities to act but were not taking advantage of them.[46] Vanderbilt University professor Dale Ballou similarly found in Massachusetts that "on virtually every issue of personnel policy, there are contracts that grant administrators the managerial prerogatives they are commonly thought to lack. . . . When more flexible language is negotiated, administrators do not take advantage of it."[47] Mitch Price of the University of Washington concluded in a 2009 study of districts in California, Ohio, and Washington that "because so many administrators, union leaders, and others perceive contracts as inflexible, the perception overtakes the reality . . . lead[ing] to practices that may be more rigid than the actual language of the contracts requires."[48]

What's going on? The vast majority of superintendents have learned to regard precedent-breaking action as risky and conflict as something to be avoided. Fully 80 percent of superintendents follow a career path that leads from teacher to principal to superintendent (with two-thirds serving in the district central office en route). Principals are almost entirely drawn from the ranks of former teachers, and almost all receive their leadership training in schools of education, where inclinations toward consensual "best practices" are frequently strengthened into dogma.

In a 2007 *Teachers College Record* study, Andrew Kelly and I examined more than 200 syllabi from a national sample of principal preparation programs and found little or no attention given to issues like eliminating ineffective programs, removing mediocre employees, using data to overhaul operations, or devising ways to use staff and services more productively.[49] The most widely assigned texts all treated education as a unique pursuit, echoing Thomas Sergiovanni's assertion that preparation for educational leadership is unlike other leadership roles and that "we [must] accept the reality that leadership for the schoolhouse should be different, and . . . we [need to] begin to invent our own practice."[50] The most commonly assigned authors included education icons like Sergiovanni, Michael Fullan, Lee Bolman, and Linda Darling-Hammond. Utterly absent were influential management thinkers like Michael Porter, Jim Collins, Clayton Christensen, and Tom Peters, who have wrestled with these issues for decades; other notable thinkers like Daniel Goleman, Peter Drucker, and Warren Bennis appeared just a half-dozen times—*combined*—out of more than 1,800 assigned readings. Superintendents who have spent their entire careers in K–12 education have had little or no exposure to different ways of leading and naturally grow to regard familiar routines as immutable.

In the course of their professional experiences, few superintendents are exposed to more assertive models of leadership or to how managers operate outside of K–12. Career superintendents are trained and socialized to pursue consensus among all interested stakeholders. Those seeking successful careers are advised to steer clear of heated clashes over staffing, school closures, new delivery models, or nontraditional vendors and instead to move deliberately on less-controversial best practice strategies. These habits of mind tend to make districts inhospitable to greenfield and leave most district leaders disinclined to help entrepreneurs find their way into the district.

Thinking Like a Greenfielder

Ted Kolderie is a founding partner of Education | Evolving, an education policy and school design shop based in Saint Paul, Minnesota, that is a national leader in greenfield thinking about redesigning teaching and learning in the 21st century and what that will require. In a 2008 report, "The Other Half of the Strategy," Kolderie argues that traditional efforts to develop "new and better approaches to learning" have fallen short and that "efforts to improve marginally are not acceptable and efforts to transform K–12 dramatically through politics are not realistic." Instead, he points to the importance of leaders creating entrepreneurial space for fresh thinking and technology rather than trying to legislate change.

Policy cannot create change. Kolderie argues that comprehensive reform efforts are doomed to failure. First, they require everyone to buy into a single model: "If we think we must have an 'agreed solution,' with everyone 'buying in' on a single model, we will not accomplish much change that is truly significant." Second, these blueprints are overly optimistic about implementation. "Occasionally someone does offer a dramatic vision that, if implemented according to the blueprint provided, would transform the system," Kolderie concedes, "but these proposals for large-scale engineered change tend not to succeed. It is beyond the capacity of our political system to impose a blueprint on dissenters or to execute it faithfully in 29 steps over the next 9 years."

Governors as gardeners. Kolderie calls for states to create "a sector in public education in which innovators . . . can try new forms of schooling; a sector structured to be congenial to innovation and in which the new and different models are protected. Public education exists in state law and, if a new space is to be created, the governors and legislatures will be the architects and implementers of the change." Kolderie gives credit to states that have enacted hospitable charter school legislation, but says there's a long way to go: "Laws need to be enacted where they do not now exist, and improved almost everywhere else. . . . But the states and the national government should work with a light touch, should keep 'the rules' minimal. For government, innovation means providing opportunities, not producer subsidies."

Fresh thinking. Kolderie says, "For new models of school and schooling we will probably need to look mainly to people new to education and now outside it." While "it can be a challenge to believe in unconventional people," Kolderie offers the example of Paul MacCready, who won the Kremer prize for human-powered flight in 1977 with a device constructed out of piano wire, bicycle parts, and Mylar. He notes that MacCready was not an aircraft structural designer, but saw that the traditional approaches of his competitors were going nowhere. MacCready relates, "Not having a background in structures permitted me to adapt some very simple-minded techniques rather than being blinded by training in structures." Kolderie adds, "There is little in our schools and our culture that forces us to get away from established patterns and look at things in different ways. . . . The conventional model of school is absolutely imprinted in our consciousness."

Technology. Kolderie argues, "We have a coincidence of need and opportunity. New technology is appearing just as the old technology is reaching its limits. This often happens. The automobile appeared just as cities needed an alternative to the horse. Business machines appeared as office filing systems broke down. Petroleum came along as whale oil disappeared. The telegraph appeared just as communication needed to cross the continent."

Kolderie explains the discontents of educational technology thusly: "Most schools now have computers; most connected to the Internet. The issue today is use. Most is 'type-one' use, adapting the new technology to present-day school—much as, early on, cinematography was used to film stage plays." Such use of technology supplements, but does not supplant, traditional classroom instruction. Ultimately, he says, "the opportunity to change school really opens up with the 'type-two' applications in which school is adapted to the characteristics and the potential of the electronics. . . . In contrast to conventional school, these offer flexibility in time and place." While adults may be wary of such radical change, Kolderie concludes, "Clearly the day is gone when the best or the only way to put young people in touch with knowledge is to send into their classroom an instructor with books under her arm."[51]

Limited Set of Greenfield Locales

Greenfield operations tend to cluster in a few communities. This is inevitable, given the political constraints that exist in most places. But it also means that a handful of locales play an outsized role. For instance, there are only eight cities—Baltimore, Chicago, Memphis, New Orleans, New York City, San Francisco, Oakland, and Washington, DC—in which Teach For America, New Leaders, and KIPP all operate. The list of truly receptive districts probably numbers fewer than a dozen.

Reliance on these few locales lends enormous influence to those who make the rules in them. Entrepreneurs must craft their proposals in ways that will not be unpalatable in the few states and districts where they find themselves accepted. This is why Edison Schools (now EdisonLearning), for instance, twisted itself into knots a few years back, altering its school design and personnel practices in order to land 20 schools in Philadelphia and take advantage of the district's interest in outsourcing the management of several dozen schools.

It is not unusual for a new entrant in any market to depend on a small number of clients, but those clients typically differ from one firm to the next. In education, the new entrants depend so heavily on the *same* few entrepreneur-friendly locales, and on the individuals who lead them, that a few personalities ultimately dictate the direction and shape of much greenfield schooling activity across the country. The reliance on a handful of critical locales also creates an environment in which Arne Duncan leaving Chicago to become U.S. secretary of education or Paul Vallas departing Philadelphia to head the Recovery School District of Louisiana can leave fragile entrepreneurs hanging by a thread.

Even in the most receptive districts, only parts of the schools and services are truly open to new providers. Chicago's hotly debated "Renaissance 2010" effort, which aimed to launch 100 new schools and shutter low-performing ones in the decade preceding 2010, has been touted nationally for its ambition.

Yet even that aggressive, decade-long effort sought to involve, at most, 20 percent of the city's 500 generally low-performing schools. What looks from a distance like a wealth of opportunities soon reduces to a handful of greenfield districts and a limited number of opportunities within them.

Conclusion

As noted in Chapter 1, the tendency of organizations to get stuck is not unique to schooling. Established organizations have trouble adapting to change, due in large part to the natural desire to placate their established constituencies. Transformative change is rarely consensual because it inevitably requires some constituencies, at least in the short term, to swallow bitter medicine. If doing better requires doing things differently, it is not just a matter of eliminating laws and rules that *prohibit* change. Greenfield also requires a culture that attracts and supports people who are *inclined* to push against familiar routines and who have the skill and experience to devise workable alternatives. A key problem in schooling is not only the dearth of such individuals but also a culture that reinforces inaction.

Existing arrangements and standard operating procedures are entrenched and defended by powerful interests. The most powerful political actors in education are the teachers unions, colleges of education, and various associations that represent district and administrative officials. For reasons both principled and selfish, these groups are inclined to be hostile to new players and to oppose reforms that would foster entrepreneurial approaches. The resulting barriers are both formal and informal, and the distinction between the two is not always clear cut.

More fundamental change requires addressing the norms, culture, behaviors, and expectations that are intertwined with, but distinct from, formal policy. Risk-averse principals, central office administrators, school boards, and superintendents have been applauded for pursuing consensus and proceeding gingerly when it comes to the rules governing personnel, procurement, and operations.

With regard to such informal barriers, it is essential at the federal, state, and local levels to promote transparency regarding what bottlenecks and obstacles exist and why. Some roadblocks may be necessary to safeguard children or tax dollars, but many simply appear to be the remnants of routine, outdated technology systems, and industrial-age collective bargaining agreements. In particular, state and district leaders must become more insistent on negotiating flexible collective bargaining agreements, striking down practices that protect mediocre teachers or vendors, developing crucial management metrics, and putting their attorneys to work figuring out what might be *done* rather than what might be *risky*. Whatever the value of formal legislative, judicial, and contractual action to expand greenfield, school systems routinely fail to test the boundaries to see how much freedom they already have.

One reason for this caution is the desire to protect students and the dictum "First, do no harm." For that reason, policing the quality of greenfield ventures looms large, and it is essential if district officials are to feel comfortable doing business differently. It is to that issue of quality control that we now turn.

4

QUALITY

OPENING THE DOOR to unproven strategies poses obvious concerns. The aim of greenfield must always be to achieve results: to find ways to improve outcomes, address unmet needs, or operate more efficiently. Lackluster ventures that sell second-rate pizza or paper towels to willing buyers present little risk to the general good. It is a different proposition when entrepreneurs are pursuing public dollars to deliver schooling or sell services or supplies to students or schools.

Serious educational entrepreneurs crave accountability and smart quality control; they are relentless in their own pursuit of results, and their viability depends on being able to demonstrate performance. Greenfield quality control is about devising smart ways to police quality that neither stifle new problem solvers nor create burdensome or heavy-handed rules or regulations. This suggests a need to empower informed educators, public officials, families, providers, and self-policing associations, rather than relying overmuch on broad accountability systems.

Public schools have traditionally pursued what passes for accountability through a thicket of state and district regulations. Licensure requirements regulate teachers and staff. Central offices dictate key school decisions, such as budget issues and personnel assignments, and monitor compliance. In many jurisdictions, textbooks and other classroom materials are subject to separate state-approval processes. And, of course, generic rules apply with regard to fire and safety norms for buildings, licensure for bus drivers and school nurses, and even bus routes and cafeteria food.

If those traditional accountability measures worked as intended—if dictating teacher credentials and how schools should be staffed actually ensured high-quality teaching and learning—greenfield schooling would be a moot point. The K–12 quality-control model was designed for a system that lacked good data on outcomes, assumed that schools would be run by large bureaucracies, and thought tracking inputs would be both efficient and equitable. This reliance on standardized processes and inputs was typical for early and mid-20th century America. Indeed, it represented the then-state-of-the-art version of best business practices and was very much part of the old "one best system" model that shaped U.S. public education.

But these outdated regulations do not ensure quality. Instead, they promote a watery mediocrity and entangle hard-charging principals, teachers, and superintendents in red tape. If we trap the new entrepreneurs in the same web, we can logically assume that the models of schooling they create will neither look much different from nor do much better than their predecessors. Fortunately, we have the ability to rethink quality control for a new era, thanks to new tools, technology, and information systems; a flood of data on outcomes; and a more sophisticated understanding of the uncertain relationship between school inputs and academic results.

The drive toward standards and accountability in recent decades has made it easier for new ventures to emerge. Accountability has identified key shortcomings that entrepreneurs can help address. For example, setting aside its many shortcomings, NCLB has spurred a willingness to consider unconventional solutions and has created opportunities for new ventures to provide supplemental education services (as discussed in Chapter 3). Although most of our public education systems were designed to focus on *inputs*, such as dollars and hours of seat time—and management processes evolved accordingly—the emphasis today is increasingly on *results*. This shift creates enormous opportunities for entrepreneurs to provide the requisite people, tools, and practices. Unfortunately, while "accountability" has become a catchword in recent years, states and districts too rarely take it to heart. Indeed, Dane Linn, director of education for the National Governors Association, notes that when states contract with providers to handle school restructuring, "very few states have any level of accountability. . . . They feel as though once they turn over the contract to an independent provider, they've fulfilled their responsibility."

The challenge is to devise smart ways to safeguard students, public dollars, and society's interests without stifling creative problem solving. Otherwise, as Chester E. Finn Jr., president of the Thomas B. Fordham Institute, has asked, "Will this goose be strangled before we can determine whether any of its eggs contain gold?"[1] If we make it easier for new providers to enter the K–12 space, launch new endeavors, and change familiar practices, it would be absurd to expect that we can monitor quality with the same old approaches. At the same time, we do not want entrepreneurs rifling public funds to pay for goods and services that fail to deliver.

The Three Approaches to Quality Control

There are three strategies for pursuing quality control: judging inputs, relying on the marketplace, and evaluating outputs. One way to think about these courses of action is in stages: what is required for an entrepreneur to get started, how he should be judged in practice, and whether he ought to be permitted to continue operating.

Input-based arrangements provide some basic assurances and are most easily understood as a set of conditions that a provider must abide by in order to operate. This process can minimize the risk of fly-by-night operations, but as Finn warns, "of course, that process can also lead to over-prescriptiveness and market-stifling by customers so fussy that few suppliers can meet their requirements."[2] Input-based systems can advantage large operators with resources and political connections while smothering new entrants. Education is full of such regulation setups, and some of them (e.g., fiscal audits, building safety inspections, and state tests) are necessary. The challenge is to collect more nuanced and useful performance information while removing the over-burdening hand of government.

We do not have to look far for models that hold promise. First, consider the kind of "self-policing" represented by the movie-rating system, college accrediting bodies, or the way state bar associations design and oversee qualifying exams for legal practice. In each case, self-interested organizations create an entity intended to signal quality and prevent the entire industry from being dragged down by shoddy providers.

The second approach relies on the invisible hand of the marketplace. Consumers (whether they are families, teachers, principals, district purchasing managers, or the like) gauge and react to quality as they make individual decisions about goods and services. Once providers are up and running, market accountability presumes that consumers will seek the information they deem useful and use it to judge competing providers. Markets create opportunities for nuanced, consumer-based decision making, but can be more or less effective depending on whether consumers can access clear, trusted, meaningful data on performance and gauge the costs and relative strengths of competing providers. In any field, undue focus on marketing, market share, or short-term gains may distract attention from quality or long-term value. Just as American International Group (AIG) for years marketed fanciful credit default swaps that were dismissed by uberinvestor Warren Buffett as a ticking time bomb, so providers may engage in misleading advertising or offer tutoring services or learning materials that do not necessarily do much good.

Vital to healthy market discipline is the availability of clear, useful information that permits consumers to compare cost and quality and to make good choices. One example of this kind of tool is the database that New Haven–based Connecticut Coalition for Achievement Now (ConnCAN) has built to help parents make smart school choices. The database compiles school-level data on student achievement, calculates the rate at which achievement scores are increasing at each school, and posts a report card on its Web site. Report cards cover over 1,000 of Connecticut's public schools and each of the state's 170 districts. In addition to achievement data, the Web site provides a profile for each school, including the number of students, basic demographic information, and per-pupil spending. The site also features simple grades that rate each school in categories, including "performance gains" and "gap between subgroups." The profiles also show how each school compares to others in the same district. This kind of information can allow parents to make savvier decisions and can promote accountability without relying on government oversight.

Parents are not the only consumers in the education marketplace. Schools and districts purchase a variety of educational technologies and services as well, but too often lack the information, expertise, or incentive to scrutinize the quality of goods or services available. This is not intended as a cheap shot. School and district leaders often do not have access to the data and metrics necessary to make good decisions. But it is also the case that they have not made cost-effectiveness and careful judgment of products and services a high priority. In most sectors, firms such as J. D. Power and Associates and Morningstar play the useful role of selling product evaluations to would-be purchasers and investors. Nobody expects individual shoppers at Wal-Mart to worry about a store's inventory software, because we trust Wal-Mart and its competitors to be smart buyers themselves, imposing market-based quality control on the goods *they* purchase and allowing consumers to ultimately benefit without having to do a thing. There are various, nongovernmental mechanisms to collect this granular information. Consider the "independent reviewer" model, in which third parties establish a business based on evaluating providers—as with Fiske's college guides, RottenTomatoes.com's movie reviews, or *Consumer Reports*'s comparisons of laptops. Some such models rely on expert reviews, others on the experiences and opinions of consumers, and others incorporate data, lab tests, or formal comparisons. These models have great promise in education to provide useful metrics and equip leaders to make a variety of distinctions on cost and quality. The third accountability mechanism is outcome-based and reliant on public officials to establish clear benchmarks for measuring results—whether student learning, recruitment or training success, or the quality of service delivery. This kind of accountability is premised on a simple truth: What you measure is what you get. The most familiar example is NCLB-style accountability, in which all schools are assessed on student reading and math proficiency in grades 3 through 8. Such metrics enable officials to loosen input regulations and offer more room for creative problem solving while still safeguarding common interests and providing a consistent way to monitor performance.

Needless to say, outcome-based accountability that is focused on student achievement is controversial, and we will not rehash the heated debates over student assessment here. As with NCLB, the outcome-accountability model implies that providers who consistently fail to meet government targets will suffer consequences (presumably, closure). Handled carelessly, however, evaluations based on standardized, crude instruments can encourage providers to narrow their efforts and can misrepresent the quality of their work. For instance, evaluating doctors primarily on how many patients they see per day might lead to hurried check-ups and compromised care. If metrics are poorly chosen or the performance targets are unrealistic, outcome-based accountability can prove counterproductive.[3]

It is worth noting, however, that at a relatively prosaic level, it is not hard to reach broad agreement about the essentials that children should be mastering. There is widespread consensus that students should at least be able to read, write, and perform mathematics with reasonable, age-appropriate proficiency, and be well versed in history and the sciences. For citizens, policymakers, or investors to be comfortable embracing entrepreneurial ventures, accurate performance measurement and meaningful quality control are essential. If school builders, tool builders, or talent providers are addressing problems in better or more cost-effective ways, they need metrics that allow them to demonstrate their edge to potential buyers.

The Promise of Value-Added Outcome Measures

Ambiguous goals and elastic criteria make it possible for schools, districts, or other providers to maintain that they are doing a good day's work whether students are learning or not. Well-designed accountability makes it possible to ultimately judge providers and educators by a clear standard, or, rather, by former President George W. Bush's famous formulation: "Is our children learning?" When we lack such measures, it is too easy for providers to shrug off disappointing outcomes and for mediocrity to be accepted as inevitable.

Unit record systems, which track student learning over time and with records that are linked to schools, teachers, and providers, allow decision makers to gauge performance and use it to hold educators and providers responsible. Performance is most usefully judged not merely by seeing who has the highest-achieving students but also by determining whose students are making the greatest progress over time. This emphasis on "value-added" assessment, when coupled with data systems that track individual students from year to year, provides the building blocks for rigorous outcome-based accountability.

Schooling is rife with debates about whether and how student achievement should be used to evaluate individual teachers. Because performance measures are imperfect and involve substantial random fluctuation in classroom-level results, these measures may be problematic for measuring teacher performance but are becoming increasingly reliable when judging the performance of larger entities. In other words, whatever one thinks about linking teacher pay to student achievement, the imperfections are much reduced when *growth* in student achievement is used to judge schools, districts, or new ventures.

More carefully gauging the benefits that schools deliver to students and society can open the door to rewarding performance in all kinds of interesting ways. For instance, the SEED Foundation's Eric Adler relates the challenge of convincing a state to invest in the program's boarding costs. One possibility they have come up with is to sign a contract with local, state, or federal government entities that promises payment in return for results—when a student graduates from high school or college, for example. As Adler puts it, "Is there a mechanism by which [we] can say to the state, 'You don't have to pay us now. . . . We'll finance it in some way, and you just pay us down the line when the results have started to materialize'?" Such a contract would essentially allow the government to invest in the project contingent upon its effectiveness, while creating a contractual stream of cash for the SEED Foundation. In turn, the SEED Foundation could turn to the private sector to securitize the anticipated cash flow and use those private funds to launch and operate the new school. Given the reality of political dynamics, such an approach lends a key role to local- and state-based entities that can forge these partnerships, provide political support, foster networks, and leverage additional dollars.

The Limits of NCLB-Style Accountability

Because we have spent the better part of a decade living under NCLB, there is a pronounced tendency to talk about accountability and quality control primarily in terms of NCLB-style testing and reporting. While such test-based metrics have an important role, their utility should not be exaggerated, and no one should imagine that NCLB-style testing is the alpha and omega of greenfield accountability.

There is real peril in overreliance on student assessments, especially the crude tests, the simplistic performance measures, and the narrow focus on reading and math in grades 3 through 8 that is enshrined in NCLB. First, such an approach targets too narrow a range of excellence. Schools or programs that do a terrific job of teaching subjects, grade levels, or skills that are not measured in state assessments are too readily overlooked. Second, the emphasis on thresholds of student achievement fails to recognize the specific value that schools or educators are adding. A focus on whether students are proficient can create an insuperable burden for programs serving disadvantaged students while giving a free pass to schools serving students who already have substantial reading and math skills. Finally, the single-minded focus on these narrowly circumscribed student outcomes means little attention is paid to other kinds of measures that more fully reflect the value of different providers—whether that is providing high-quality data systems or helping districts fix broken human resource departments.

One unfortunate consequence of NCLB-style accountability and its focus on reading and math scores in grades 3 through 8 has been a tendency to drive energy, attention, and focus toward trying to mimic the "best practices" of high-performing schools—with all the usual limitations discussed in Chapter 1. And so, not surprisingly, most successful new school models have been those focused on basic skills in grades 3 through 8. At the same time, it has been much more difficult for tool builders, human capital providers, or schools focused on nontested populations (such as K–2 or high school students) to demonstrate their effectiveness and generate interest.

Greenfield quality control must start from a much broader basis, asking, "What kinds of measures might accurately reflect and usefully address performance without stifling creative problem solving among school builders, tool builders, or talent providers?" The answer surely begins with the realization that not everything can be measured with the same set of metrics. Smart quality control does not necessarily lead to simple "yes/no" decisions about whether a school or product "works" but provides a floor for gauging product quality and guides consumers in determining the performance and value of their options.

For instance, *Consumer Reports* often suggests "best buys" in several price ranges; whether the $4,000 or the $1,500 flat-screen TV is a "best buy" for a given family will depend on the family's budget, preferences, and desired features. This is not dissimilar to the plight of superintendents trying to choose between alternative math curricula or SES tutoring. However, it is quite different from the case of parents selecting public school options, as their out-of-pocket costs will be identical—zero, in every case—because all the money is provided by the government. The bottom line is that some quality-control strategies work better for some goods and services, in some contexts, and for some users. The criteria for gauging whether a professional development provider is cost-effective are different from those that can help indicate whether a school should adopt a particular online calculus course. Yet we have focused in the past decade on developing just one set of metrics. The greenfield starting point for sensible measuring and monitoring is to do a better job of tracking the right metrics; this requires not just high-tech data systems but ones that are smart and well designed as well.

Smart Data Systems

Measuring the full range of data needed for good decisions and quality control requires public and private organizations to design and adopt the kind of robust "balanced scorecards" that leading public and private organizations have used for decades. Balanced scorecards measure not just how an organization does overall (e.g., how students do on assessments) but also how well employees perform their various roles (e.g., how rapidly maintenance responds to a teacher's request or how highly new teachers rate their instructional coach). Balanced scorecards require collecting and analyzing data about crucial operational processes, such as teacher recruitment and placement, textbook delivery, and professional development. Tracking such data in real time exposes inefficiencies, equips leaders to make good decisions, and identifies areas where entrepreneurial problem solving is most sorely needed.[4]

Mark Vineis, founder of Mondo Publishing, a New York City–based educational publisher of literacy resources and provider of professional development services, explains how this plays out in practice. In the course of more than two decades, Vineis has observed that "the 'management' of reform policies often stops with the articulation of the reform mandate from the central office, in the belief that the mandate equals implementation." Too often, Vineis notes, "data points for even the most 'basic routines,' such as specific times that teachers meet for focused professional learning or the exact schedule for the literacy block in each classroom, are not readily available." The result is an inability to know what's working, what schools are actually doing, or what kind of support schools require.

In some bright spots, however, district leadership is approaching data more strategically and working with partners to develop essential metrics and data systems. In Colorado, Aurora Public Schools superintendent John Barry, a former Air Force general, has erected metrics to support and monitor day-to-day instruction and adult professional learning at each school. Vineis observes that in doing so, Barry has been able "to better link the realities of each classroom and school to the superintendent and his leadership team." Ultimately, student achievement data alone yield only a "black box," illustrating how students are faring but not enabling an organization to *diagnose* problems or *manage* improvement. The result is "data-driven" systems that encourage leaders to give short shrift to the operations, hiring, and financial practices that are the backbone of well-run organizations. For a terrific example of how this information is used by smart educators at three respected charter management organizations (Uncommon Schools, Aspire Public Schools, and Leadership Public Schools), see Figure 4.1, which illustrates the kinds of metrics and analyses that these organizations use to track academic, financial, and operational performance.

Remarkably few districts track how long it takes human resources to respond to a teaching applicant, how frequently teachers utilize formative assessment, or how rapidly the central office processes and fulfills requests for supplies. Data-driven management requires tracking an array of indicators, such as how long it takes books and materials to be shipped to classrooms, whether schools provide students with accurate (and appropriate) schedules in a timely fashion, the turnaround time on assessment data, and the frequency with which these data are utilized.

For all of our attention to testing and assessment, student achievement measures reflect the performance of many school district personnel only indirectly and over the course of time. Just as hospitals employ large numbers of administrative and clinical personnel to support doctors, so schools have a "long tail" of support staff charged with ensuring that educators have the tools they need to be effective. Just as it makes no sense to judge the quality of army chefs on the outcome of combat operations, so it makes no sense to judge the performance of a school's payroll personnel on student test results. In place of our relentless focus on statewide, formal metrics that can be imposed in cookie-cutter fashion, what districts and providers need are data that reflect the quality of their work and position them to identify both strengths and areas for improvement.

Tim Daly, CEO of The New Teacher Project, observes that blunt metrics make it more difficult for districts to grasp or accurately judge the value of the talent his organization provides. When marketing TNTP's services to districts with substantial staffing needs, he says, a great concern is that districts "don't think critically about the relative importance of each hire."

Figure 4.1
Data Dashboards at Three Charter Management Organizations

	Type of Dashboard	Metrics	Method	Frequency	Audiences
UNCOMMON	*Academic*	• Interim assessments (compared to last year's cohort at same grade/subject; not disaggregated by specific subgroups) • Student attrition (month to month) • Enrollment and attendance • Demographics (mostly for external audiences)	• Data are disaggregated by schools. • Results are not compared to specific targets, but implicit goals that measures will improve each year.	Quarterly	Home office management team, Board
ASPIRE	*Operational*	• Enrollment • Wait list and attrition/transfers out • Attendance • Financial	• Data are disaggregated by schools. • Results are compared to targets set each quarter.	Every 1–2 months	Home office management team, Board
	Academic	• Interim assessments	• Data are disaggregated by schools. • Results are compared to targets set each quarter.	Every 1–2 months	Home office management team, Board
	Financial	• Average Daily Attendance (ADA) • Enrollment • Free/reduced lunch • Supplemental hours	• Data are disaggregated by schools. • Results are compared to target goals based on the previous quarter.	Monthly	Home office management team, Board
	Operational	• Staff-recruitment pipeline	• Results are compared to target goals based on the previous quarter.	Quarterly	Home office management team, Board
LEADERSHIP	*Academic*	• Interim assessments	• Data are disaggregated across schools. • Results are not compared to specific targets.	Quarterly	Home office management team, Board, Principals

Source: "Performance Dashboards" (p. 6) in *Practices From the Portfolio, Volume 2,* 2008, San Francisco: NewSchools Venture Fund. © 2008 by NewSchools Venture Fund. Reprinted with permission.

He explains:

> Elementary teachers are typically easy to find—even without recruiting them, a district will get a steady supply. TNTP tends to recruit math and science teachers that would not be available to a district without intensive cultivation and broad outreach. And districts don't account for the cost or the academic impact of positions that never get filled. For instance, a district might hire 400 teachers at [their average cost per hire], but 100 vacancies might not get filled at all, and those classrooms would be filled with subs. Filling the last hundred vacancies is going to cost a lot more than filling the first hundred, especially if they are in high-poverty schools. In short, we found that districts did not have cost-calculation tools that would enable them to make rational decisions about teacher pipelines.

No one is suggesting that districts necessarily should hire TNTP or that TNTP is offering every district an attractive or cost-effective solution. The point, rather, is that districts with good cost and staffing data will be better equipped to sensibly judge what TNTP has to offer, and they will also have a clearer view of inefficient operations that hamper educators and make it hard for new ventures to win a fair hearing.

Five Key Questions

Given the variety of possible methods of quality control, there is no single right set of metrics for every school. School leaders must determine which approaches make sense in their situation, and broad criteria must be available to guide policymakers, practitioners, parents, and funders. Chester E. Finn Jr., president of the Thomas Fordham Institute, has spelled out five questions that provide a terrific starting point for these deliberations:

- Does it (the provider, intervention, specialized program, etc.) do what it claims to do? That is, does it actually provide the service it promises for (where appropriate) the price that it states?
- Is there evidence of cost-effectiveness? Is it worth the money? This may matter less for parent consumers of public education (who are spending taxpayers' funds), but it is certainly a question for districts or schools that must stay within budget when procuring goods and services.
- Is there reliable evidence (preferably from trustworthy third parties) that it accomplishes what it claims? In many instances, this would include evidence of enhanced student learning, but different evidence may be better suited to other kinds of providers (e.g., food services and data management).

- How reliable and consistent (and replicable) is it from one place to another, and how much does its performance depend on specific and thus variable implementation?
- What are its strengths and weaknesses compared to other providers of kindred services?[5]

If we could answer these questions appropriately for any given entrepreneur, service, program, or intervention, we would be far better off. Indeed, one might imagine that district leaders and entrepreneurs in such a world would enjoy enormous latitude to pursue smart reinvention, with parents and policymakers confident that the decisions and handiwork of greenfield operators would be transparent and appropriately monitored.

Quality Control on the Front End

Our old friend Matt Candler left the KIPP Academies in 2004 to take up the post of chief operating officer with a new outfit: the New York City Center for Charter School Excellence. At the Center, he drew on his work at KIPP to pioneer new strategies for pursuing quality control in the charter sector. His recollections provide a fascinating firsthand take on what purposive quality control can look like in the entrepreneurial space.

Candler joined the Center under CEO Paula Gavin, who was a former CEO of the YMCA and well equipped to serve as the public face of the Center's effort. Candler and Gavin started visiting the city's charter schools to meet educators and explain what they were going to do with the $40 million in funding they had at their disposal. Candler recalls, "Those early visits were critical for the Center, as we established up front that we were about quality in charters, not about charters alone. We would not protect weak schools. In fact, we pleaded for school leaders to self-police and put pressure on one another. This proactive stance was a departure from most traditional charter support efforts, and one that we worked hard to communicate." Most people in the charter school world found this approach highly unusual and thought the Center to be, in Candler's words, "an old-school charter school resource center on steroids." Resource centers had historically helped pass charter legislation in a given state and focused on getting schools approved. Their mission was to help applicants navigate the charter approval process, leaving questions of quality either to the school leadership or the "authorizer" responsible for chartering the school.

Candler saw his mission differently. "I was obsessed with destroying the perception of being a resource center," he says. "I wanted to build a team of seasoned and accomplished educators . . . to get control of the pipeline and put KIPP-like practices in place, both in terms of picking quality operators and getting them ready for opening day." He aimed to make the Center "attractive enough to all applicants to have them want to work with us" and then to cherry-pick "the very best of that group." Twice a year, the Center hosted free sessions to explain the basics of starting charter schools, at which staff took pains to make sure attendees understood how tough it was. Those efforts helped screen possible applicants and identified strong prospective school founders, whom Center staff would then either steer to submit applications or to hold off, if the staff thought the individuals were not yet prepared.

Candler's quality-control strategy had three key components. The first was to seek strong candidates; the second was doing early, initial quality screening; and the third was to support and nurture new ventures. He recollects, "After the free sessions, Jessica Nauiokas [who led the screening effort] would get to work with those still interested in pursuing the new school idea. She would ask them to fill out a simple technical-assistance application, our first screening device. If approved, they would be eligible for $10,000 worth of free startup advice. This was not a grant, but it was free help provided by hired consultants working on loan to us. We checked in monthly with our team of consultants and asked them to steer the most promising toward applying to the authorizer for a school and to the Center for a larger, more intensive $35,000 planning grant. We asked each consultant to mine less-promising groups for individual talent that might be ready someday."

Candler explains, "We were willing to lose the $35,000 investment in a school if during that grant period we learned a school was not up to the challenge. This was a simple cost-benefit calculation for us: $35,000 was a small price to pay to keep a bad school off the street. We did not do it often, but it only took one or two to send a message."

Once schools were formally approved, they applied for $50,000 post-approval startup grants, and the founding team was introduced to similarly situated "teammates," providing a network and community of mutual support as they tackled the operational and instructional challenges of launching a new school. Candler explains that these grants were intended to provide "the same kind of support to schools that blazers used to provide at KIPP. We asked schools to use part of their startup grant to hire operations directors early in the year. This paid off, as our grant recipients entered the school year with strong financial and operational controls." This enabled these schools to avoid the logistical headaches that plague so many charters and to focus intently from day one on delivering high-quality instruction and on building a focused school culture.[6]

The National Association of Charter School Authorizers (NACSA) is charged with working to ensure that all charter schools operate under this kind of rigorous quality control. Under the charter model, the legislature empowers "authorizers" (which can be school districts, mayors, colleges, or just about any entity the legislature chooses) to approve new charter schools and screen out weak applicants, oversee ongoing performance, and evaluate schools to make renewal decisions and close those schools that are underperforming. The challenge for authorizers is to find ways to simultaneously support quality and entrepreneurial growth—especially when most authorizers are school districts that have shown little commitment to charter schooling, and many others have not demonstrated the will or capacity to promote excellence.

As the national association of more than 700 authorizers, NACSA has advocated policies and practices that set clear and challenging requirements for new charter schools, provide for meaningful and reliable metrics to track the performance of existing schools, and result in the quick and conclusive closure of lousy schools. NACSA has self-interested reasons to champion strong authorizers and put pressure on mediocre ones. In that position, NACSA not only provides guidance and leadership but also plays an active role on the ground to bolster authorizing in "priority" states, including Louisiana, Ohio, and Florida. While it is far from clear that NACSA will be successful, its efforts offer one welcome avenue.

More broadly, these examples make clear the importance of employing sensible metrics and providing honest assessments about school performance. When it comes to charter schooling and school choice, there has been a tendency to simply assume that creating choices will translate into quality control. The NACSA strategy, when executed properly, looks worlds different from how we traditionally address quality control in the realm of school choice and charter schooling. On the other hand, it looks *very* similar to ways in which smart, diligent investors in Silicon Valley decide which new ventures to back.

The Power of Branding

Branding offers another powerful but rarely used approach to accountability and quality control. When self-interest, survival, and success depend on reputation, there is an enormous incentive to measure, police, and demonstrate quality. The branding imperative has been only weakly evident in schooling, but it is a powerful lever for greenfield quality control. Firms that many of us in schooling routinely mock as soulless, buck-chasing corporations—think McDonald's or Subway—move swiftly to intervene if franchises are damaging their brand or making unauthorized alterations to the corporate model. Indeed, corporate America, for all its flaws, exercises relatively effective internal quality control. That is why we take for granted a reasonably predictable experience at any one of a thousand Starbucks. Wal-Mart, Burger King, and Gap inspect their own stores, monitor their own products, and ferret out problems because failing to do so jeopardizes their success and viability. Hotel chains like Hilton and Marriott send anonymous inspectors to check on cleanliness and service.

In the private sector, when successful businesses want to maintain quality while expanding, they choose between two models: corporate-style growth with central management or franchising. Chains such as Starbucks scale up via corporate management; each of that company's nearly 10,000 U.S. outlets is owned and managed from the firm's Seattle headquarters. Other firms, such as McDonald's, have employed a franchising model, which allows firms to leverage the talent and resources of eager applicants rather than requiring that all the talent and money be supplied by the existing firm. Franchisees pay an annual royalty back in return for use of the brand, products, and support services. In education, that kind of branding could serve as a quick, user-friendly quality assurance for parents trying to choose a good school, or for district officials trying to decide whether to hire a talent provider. Of course, the franchising model inevitably poses new challenges in policing quality, since the organization is leasing its name and reputation to a quasi-independent operator.

In K–12 schooling, KIPP is the best-known practitioner of the franchise model. Each KIPP school pays roughly 1 percent of its state and local funding to the nonprofit KIPP Foundation. If a school does not meet KIPP's standards, the KIPP Foundation retains the right to withdraw its support and the school's ability to use the KIPP name. Since KIPP started replicating schools in 2001, 7 of 73 schools have closed or left its network. Of the seven, three schools—in Atlanta, Buffalo, and Edgewater, Maryland—were dropped for not meeting KIPP's standards, lack of financial stability, or inability to secure a school facility. Two KIPP schools merged with a second school, primarily due to low enrollment. And two additional schools separated from KIPP for philosophical reasons or because they sought more local control.

Business writer Julie Bennett, author of *Franchise Times Guide to Selecting, Buying, & Owning a Franchise*, has noted that other charter management organizations (CMOs) have adopted a more centralized management model. The CEO of the Massachusetts-based Lighthouse Academies, for instance, has reported that he tightly controls the organization's 11 schools and is "literally in every school at least once a month."[7] Lighthouse schools all look alike, with the same blue and yellow walls, and employ the same instructional programs. On the other hand, New Haven, Connecticut–based Achievement First does not pursue the same kind of uniformity. Instead, says CEO Doug McCurry, its 15 schools emphasize "common benchmarks, a common scope, and an emerging set of best practices" and receive "robust back office" support, but have more freedom when it comes to school design and instruction.[8]

While there are stark differences between K–12 education and sectors where franchises are more common, some key lessons for quality control are clear. First, successful operations carefully pick and train their franchisees. KIPP has learned this lesson well. Applicants to its yearlong Fisher Fellowship leadership training program must have four years of teaching experience and then compete with 500 other applicants to be one of a dozen fellows. Second, successful franchisors grow carefully, providing specific instructions for new franchisees to follow. Third, they take care to refine their models before seeking to replicate. Finally, the most successful franchisors have historically tackled one geographic region or locale at a time.

Unlike stand-alone schools or bureaucratically managed districts, charter management chains have enormous incentives to protect their brand and bolster a reputation for quality. Districts can take for granted that local students will enroll in their schools, but charter networks fret that one weak link can damage the reputation of all their schools and jeopardize enrollment. Julie Bennett has observed, "Franchisors must protect the value of their brands by terminating franchisees who fail to maintain the system's quality. The franchise-model CMOs have built in some safeguards: day-to-day decisions are managed by an entrepreneurial principal who has the flexibility to change programs that may not be working [and] to expand those that are. KIPP sends an inspection team of financial, academic, real estate, and legal personnel to each new school on an annual basis."[9]

Done well, brands and franchises are powerful tools for ensuring quality and consistency within school networks. Such chains are able to focus on doing one thing well rather than trying to serve the full array of needs in a given community. They are able to provide the support systems and quality control that clear away barriers and equip new franchisees to succeed. Reformers, practitioners, and parents would do well to welcome responsible franchisees as a promising lever for serving students and addressing challenges that appear beyond the ken of local schools and districts.

Conclusion

While we have made progress in the last decade in embracing certain metrics like student performance in reading and math, we have too often turned a blind eye to the limits of such measures. Yes, standardized assessments are a valuable gauge of student learning and offer a crucial basis for comparing providers. To date, accountability efforts—particularly the 800-pound gorilla of NCLB-style testing—have created an opportunity and appetite for some kinds of ventures. But ensuring the high-quality provision of services requires operational measures and data well beyond those of student achievement.

Achievement measures are irrelevant to many educational providers or district employees. The criteria for appraising professional development or data analysis will be quite different from those that determine what Web-based foreign language course a school should provide or which local school a parent should select. Quality-control metrics need to focus on outcomes, but those outcomes cannot, and should not, simply be reading and math test scores. Whether developed by entrepreneurs trying to sell their wares or by school leaders trying to ensure they partner with only the best possible ventures, metrics need to fully and accurately reflect the work and value that recruiters, tool builders, school builders, support personnel, and school staff deliver.

Many greenfield enthusiasts have assumed that creating choices will invariably be accompanied by attention to quality. But as charter schooling has reminded us, markets offer no guarantee that consumers will insist on quality or reliably be able to judge between better and worse providers. When it comes to school builders or tool builders, as in any field, the quality of choices will depend on the caliber of available information. Bad or incomplete information, whether in the hands of parents or educators, will lead to poor decisions and too often excuse mediocrity. Even savvy parents making good choices will provide quality control only for school operators; this will do little to address the challenge for tool builders, human capital providers, or even nontraditional school providers.

Markets are a powerful but limited mechanism for promoting quality. In many fields, we happily tolerate market imperfections because we view these as a small price to pay for variety and innovation. In education, we—school builders, especially—are much more squeamish about approaches that may yield uneven quality (even if we quietly tolerate massive mediocrity and unevenness among existing school districts). One promising way to forestall overregulation is the kind of quality assurance provided by the New York City Center for Charter School Excellence and the kind of tough, results-oriented authorization championed by the National Association of Charter School Authorizers. This kind of smart quality control and public reporting by independent entities can foster an information-rich, quality-conscious ecosystem while blunting support for heavy-handed government intervention.

A number of intriguing quality-control models are worth exploring. Like the Food and Drug Administration, the Department of Education's What Works Clearinghouse reviews reading and math programs with an eye toward evidence of effectiveness. Yet the Clearinghouse is not intended to be a regulatory agency, and its approval is not mandatory. Indeed, it is closer to a *Consumer Reports* model than to formal drug approval. "Inspectors" provide monitoring that cannot readily be counted or gleaned from outcome statistics, accounting figures, or compliance reports. They can provide constructive feedback or immediate policing, such as when the health inspector shuts down a restaurant that falls short of hygienic standards. "Wiki" methods, such as those utilized by Amazon or eBay, allow consumers to provide feedback on experiences with particular providers or services and make it possible to capture and aggregate a wealth of telling information.

Although there is a pleasing simplicity to old-style regulation that clearly distinguishes the permissible from the impermissible and the satisfactory from the unsatisfactory, smart quality control acknowledges the reality of gray areas and subtle distinctions. Creating greenfield requires pursuing new public and private approaches that produce useful metrics, provide appropriate monitoring, and support thoughtful quality assurance.

5

TALENT

TALENT IS A CRITICAL INGREDIENT in any organization. The success of greenfield ventures depends on the entrepreneurs' own talent, the talent they can recruit and nurture, and their ability to maximize the talent they have. In schooling, where four out of every five dollars go to fund salaries and benefits for more than 6 million employees, there is no more important task.

Doing better first requires unlearning long-held assumptions about school staffing, including the way educators are recruited, trained, and compensated; the way faculty time is organized; and the way faculty are allocated. Second, it requires abandoning the notion that technology and investments in talent should supplement existing staffing and presuming instead that they are most valuable when they upend routines and dramatically enhance productivity. Third, and intertwined with both of these, is the challenge of attracting and nurturing entrepreneurial talent in the world of K–12 schooling.

All of these elements of greenfield are at odds with the way we usually discuss teacher quality and personnel policy in education. When we think about improving the way we recruit and retain teachers, we typically focus on improving training in teacher colleges, expanding mentoring programs, adopting modest merit pay programs, and relying heavily on best practice strategies. From a greenfield perspective, these tactics are self-defeating. It is hard to see how even souped-up versions of existing approaches will recruit or prepare the kind of talent needed to fundamentally improve K–12 education.

There are approximately 3.3 million K–12 teachers in the United States, representing nearly 10 percent of the college-educated workforce. Our schools are in a constant, unending race to annually recruit and then retain some 200,000 teachers.[1] The "more, better" mind-set has made this an even greater challenge. A steady reduction in the pupil/teacher ratio—from 22.3 students per teacher in 1970 to 15.5 students per teacher in 2006—means that the teaching force has expanded 50 percent faster than student enrollment over that time.[2] This has diluted the talent pool and suppressed salaries. It's also made it harder to deliver high-quality professional development, as investing in more teachers, rather than rewarding and providing additional training to good ones, has absorbed vast new sums. Meanwhile, best practice strategies frequently imply or even presume that we can improve teacher effectiveness by using the existing professional development machinery to improve training and mentoring.

Sometimes overlooked is the degree to which high-performing schools and districts owe their success to the ability to attract talented recruits. This "hire the best" strategy works well enough for a limited number of schools or districts that can attract the pick of the new teaching litter or can raid talent from less-prestigious neighboring districts, but such reshuffling does not do much to increase the overall number of successful schools. The real need is to devise strategies that grow the pool of effective educators—whether that involves attracting more talented recruits; creating new roles; or adopting training, systems, or technology that make practitioners more efficient.

For two decades, potentially promising proposals to address the talent challenge have run afoul of teacher colleges, collective bargaining provisions, dysfunctional human resources departments and hiring systems, cultural norms, entrenched teachers unions, and class-size mandates. The need is for ventures that can not only sketch solutions but also execute them.

Trends in the Profession

School districts have hired ever more teachers—and have asked them each to do the same job in roughly the same way as their predecessors 50 or 100 years ago. Dramatic gains in quality or productivity depend on our ability to rethink the fundamentals of the teaching profession by taking advantage of the talent we have, competing for better talent, and attracting and cultivating individuals equipped to be entrepreneurial problem solvers.

Today's profession is the product of a mid-20th century labor model that relied on a captive pool of female labor and assumed that educators were largely interchangeable. Preparation programs were geared to train generalists who operated with little access to student-level achievement data, few ways to measure the quality of goods and services, and limited opportunity to leverage new technologies. Teaching has clung to these industrial rhythms, but that model no longer works in the brain-based labor market of the 21st century.

Today, talented, energetic college graduates no longer automatically queue up to climb the corporate ladder, and accomplished young professionals are far more likely to veer from the beaten path. Schools have been slow to adjust to this changing labor market. Women, for whom teaching would have once been the default occupation, have increasingly found jobs in engineering and the law. Meanwhile, new recruits have become less likely to make teaching their lifelong career. As we noted in Chapter 3, it was not until the late 1980s that education policymakers started tinkering with alternative licensure and mid-career recruitment. Even then, they did little or nothing to redesign professional development, compensation, or career opportunities. Even today's "cutting-edge" proposals still assume that we need to fill the 200,000-a-year hiring quota with talented 22-year-olds who will line up for teaching jobs that they will hopefully hold into the late 2030s or 2040s. That is not the way most college-educated 22-year-olds approach the workforce today—especially not those who are the most energetic or have strong academic backgrounds.

Meanwhile, the nation relies on individual principals and district administrators to manage this workforce. As we saw in Chapter 3, it is too often the case that the experience and training of school leaders leaves them ill-equipped to address stubborn challenges in new or more promising ways. One notable response is that of New Leaders for New Schools, which we encountered in Chapter 3. Since it launched in 2000, NLNS has recruited and prepared more than 600 principals while accepting fewer than 7 percent of its applicants. All of NLNS's principals have prior teaching experience, but half come from partner districts and the other half from nontraditional venues, like companies, nonprofits, the military, and universities. Boasting a model that features intensive mentoring and a yearlong residency, NLNS has attracted a diverse population (nearly two-thirds African American and Latino) while assiduously tracking performance and posting promising results.

The search for talent is not unique to education. Plenty of other organizations are wooing the same smart, educated, energetic, and committed individuals. A few years ago, the consulting firm McKinsey & Company drew attention to the ongoing "war for talent" in a landmark study of more than 10,000 executives in 120 large U.S. companies.[3] It noted the fierce competition for the limited pool of "smart, sophisticated" workers who are "technologically literate, globally astute, and operationally agile."[4] McKinsey reported that "companies scoring in the top quintile of talent-management practices outperform their industry's mean return to shareholders by a remarkable 22 percentage points. Talent management is not the only driver of such performance, but it is clearly a powerful one."[5]

With that advantage in mind, Christopher Gergen and Gregg Vanourek, founders of New Mountain Ventures, have identified five important trends for reformers to keep in mind if they hope to attract a new generation of talent. First, competition for talent has led organizations to embrace creative recruiting tactics, robust investments in development and empowerment programs, and sophisticated retention efforts. World-class firms take systematic pains to shape training, corporate culture, professional opportunities, and pay in a way that will attract and energize valued employees. Second, the rise of "knowledge workers" has gained enormous momentum in the age of the Internet. While information workers made up a third of workers in 1930, they constitute up to four-fifths of the workforce today.[6] Third, today's workers are much more mobile than they were 50 years ago. In the 1960s, the U.S. Bureau of Labor Statistics reported that the typical college graduate could expect to hold five jobs in the course of his or her lifetime. That same graduate today can expect to hold four jobs by the age of 30, and the average job tenure for wage and salary earners is just four years. Finally, post–baby boomers are demanding improved "work/life balance" and work that promises social significance and impact.[7]

All of this adds up to a world in which K–12 schools must compete fiercely for the people they want. Author Richard Florida has termed the rapidly growing, highly educated, and well-paid segment of society that values individuality and merit "the creative class." Florida has calculated that this population encompasses nearly 40 million Americans, or almost a third of the workforce—up from perhaps 10 percent in the early 20th century.[8] Happily, K–12 is well-positioned to embrace educated individuals eager for work that matters—or at least it would be, if it freed itself from industrial-model hiring systems, job descriptions, and career trajectories repellent to 21st century talent. After all, Teach For America now draws applications from more than 10 percent of the graduating classes of some Ivy League schools and is more difficult to get into than Harvard Law School. One important challenge is simply to find ways to take advantage of willing talent. Today, it is too often the case that if a retired NASA scientist were to show up at the local school and inquire about teaching science, the best we might hope for from even a proactive district is that she would be enlisted as a "reading buddy" or hall monitor.

Getting into the Talent Business

Devising better ways to recruit and develop talent is critical. Some education thinkers, including influential figures like Thomas Sergiovanni and Marilyn Cochran-Smith, suggest that K–12 schooling is unique and that trying to learn about recruiting or professional training from other sectors constitutes a misguided attempt to import "business thinking." Such a take is problematic on two counts. First, a greenfielder believes that we are not currently getting the job done in K–12 and is happy to look elsewhere for good ideas. Second, as we noted in Chapter 1, today's K–12 hiring and talent practices already stem from "business thinking"; the problem is that they reflect business thinking that was state-of-the-art close to a century ago. The truth is that educators have much to learn from their colleagues in other fields.

Chasing a Moving Target

The composition of the teaching force is changing. In 1991, 70 percent of high school teachers had entered the profession by age 25, and the number entering the profession after age 35 was just 6 percent. According to the most recent data available, close to half of teachers are entering teaching after age 25, and nearly one in five is starting after age 35.[9] The transience of recent college graduates, coupled with the increasing prevalence of mid-career transitions, makes it foolhardy to try to identify future teachers at age 20, fully train them before they enter the profession, and then expect graduates to remain in teaching jobs until the 2040s.

Meanwhile, there is a large population of college-educated adults, well into their careers, who are seeking more meaningful and engaging work. A 2008 survey by the Woodrow Wilson National Fellowship Foundation reported that 42 percent of college-educated adults would consider becoming a teacher. Those interested in teaching were more academically accomplished than those who were not. And working adults who transfer laterally into teaching have more life experience, wisdom, and leadership than the average new college graduate.[10] At the same time, recruiting more mature entrants could actually reduce attrition. The National Center for Education Information has concluded, "Individuals who have entered teaching through alternate routes at older ages are more inclined to stay in teaching for longer than people entering teaching in their early-to-late 20s and 30s."[11]

This all recommends abandoning the assumption that most new teachers will or should be new college graduates and demands that we rethink the certification requirements that impede mid-career professionals from entering teaching.

Saying YES to Talent

Chris Barbic is founder and CEO of Houston-based YES Prep, a charter management organization that operates five campuses and serves 2,600 urban students. YES has been ranked the best public school in Houston by *Newsweek, U.S. News & World Report*, and the *Houston Chronicle*, and, for eight consecutive years, all of YES's graduating seniors have been accepted into four-year colleges.

Barbic recalls, "When we opened our charter in 1998, we fundamentally believed in the importance of having a great teacher in every single classroom. With only one school, it was relatively easy to find three or four 'rock star' teachers who we could hire and then stay out of their way. Once we made the commitment to open more schools, [though], we knew this approach would no longer work. . . . We would need to develop our own teachers."

He explains how they went about doing just that. "We administered a personality profile on the highest-performing quartile of teachers, along with the lowest. We selected teachers based on student achievement data and observation notes. Through these profiles, we learned that our best teachers shared some common traits that we did not see in our lowest-performing teachers."

In particular, Barbic and his team identified seven qualities:

(1) *Rebound time*—the amount of time we require to recover from a crisis or setback; (2) *energy mode*—the degree to which we prefer staying active and on the move versus stationary at work; (3) *leadership*—the extent to which we want to take responsibility for directing, controlling, coaching, delegating, and orchestrating the tasks of others; (4) *agreement*—ideal YES Teachers may show great interest in the other's needs and may be excellent listeners, but, at the end of the day, will likely only agree to the other's needs if it is conducive to success; (5) *perfectionism*—the degree to which we strive for perfection; (6) *reserve*—ideal YES Teachers tend to provide

opinion outputs on a regular basis, whether asked for or not; and (7) *drive*—how pushed we feel to continually set and achieve goals . . . [and] crave achievement. Crucially, the YES team did not seek to distill a scientifically compelling rationale or to derive a standard screening process that could be used in any school. Their task was made manageable precisely because they sought only to identify the traits that would make for successful teachers in YES schools.

Barbic adds, "Applicants are screened by a behavioral interview tool that we use to ensure candidates are a 'culture' fit with YES Prep." If applicants make it through, he says, "They are required to conduct a sample lesson in front of a group of our students [and with] the school director and dean of instruction present." Afterwards, the debriefing includes soliciting feedback from the students about the lesson and instruction.

Attracting Talent

On-campus recruiting, handsome compensation packages, and headhunters are now common among private-sector organizations seeking college-educated talent. Competitors up their ante and appeal to the heartstrings of top recruits by emphasizing culture, team spirit, and mission. This particular appeal is tailor-made for K–12 education. Gergen and Vanourek note, "Education organizations begin with an inherent advantage: the mission of education is closely aligned with the values of rising generations of professionals and emerging leaders eager to engage in meaningful work and make a difference. In that sense, talent recruitment teams in education are beginning on the 'fifty-yard line.' "[12] Yet this mind-set is barely evident in district human resources departments.

Far too many schools and districts instead find a frightening alchemy of ways to turn a passionate vocation into a rote desk job. Nearly a decade ago, Kaya Henderson, now deputy chancellor to Michelle Rhee in the DC Public Schools, was with The New Teacher Project when she approached then-DCPS superintendent Paul Vance and insisted the district could recruit 100 new mid-career professionals into teaching. Henderson recalls Vance saying, "There's no way that you'll get 100 people to come and teach in DC public schools." So TNTP launched its effort, featuring a brochure that declared, "Three out of four of our 3rd graders can't read at grade level. What can you do to help?" Henderson remembers what happened next. "Literally, we got 2,500 applicants for 100 positions," she says. "At that point, Dr. Vance said, 'OK, clearly you all know something that we don't know. Take over all of my teacher recruitment.' And so, for seven years, in addition to running DC Teaching Fellows, we worked with DC Public Schools and a number of other school districts across the country to help them rethink how they recruit and retain not just their alternatively certified candidates, but all of their candidates."[13]

Organizations that earn a reputation for pursuing excellence can make themselves magnets for talent. This is one reason why K–12 ventures like YES Prep, High Tech High, and Aspire can find themselves with dozens of talented applicants for an opening even as neighboring school districts struggle to find enough qualified applicants. Outside of K–12, Google offers an instructive example. Through a massive recruitment campaign, Google lured top executives and engineers away from attractive competitors like Microsoft, Apple, eBay, and Amazon, despite a highly selective hiring process that has been termed "grueling."[14] One of Google's attractions was its precept: "Great just isn't good enough." Such a standard tells employees that their best efforts are recognized and valued. Google values not only intelligence and aptitude but also nonconformity, with preference given to recruits with unconventional experiences and worldviews.[15] These measures have helped make the company a coveted destination for elite, tech-savvy talent.

Successful organizations differentiate themselves by helping employees see the firm as unique, even when employees are engaged in seemingly mundane activities like producing food. Consider Clif Bar, a leading producer of organic nutrition bars, which aggressively promotes itself as a health-conscious, outdoorsy brand. The firm offers sabbaticals; a wellness program that includes an in-house gym, full-time trainers, and 20 fitness classes per week; flex-time that allows employees to take three-day weekends; and a robust community service program with the goal that each employee does over 20 hours of paid volunteer work per year. The firm also donates 1 percent of annual sales to charities and appeals to its California-based, environmentally conscious workforce through a sustainability initiative led by a staff ecologist.[16] These measures attract recruits while strengthening bonds that link employees to the organization's mission and culture.

Developing Talent

Of course, it is not just about finding talent; it is also about preparing employees to excel. Wendy Kopp, who founded Teach For America when fresh out of college, recalls learning this lesson the hard way:

Although our organizational structure was based on some underlying philosophy, my approach to finding and managing staff was not. I had no idea what to look for in potential staff members. Of course they had to share a deep enthusiasm for our mission, but what else? I lucked into hiring some exceptional people in that first year, but I also picked a few who were less good fits. To make matters worse, I assumed that everyone would simply come through with little or no instruction. When staff members didn't perform at the necessary level, I concluded that they weren't cut out for the job. It never occurred to me that *I* was doing something wrong or that my inexperienced staff members needed more guidance or development.[17]

As Kopp notes, recruiting talent is only half the battle; training and development are equally crucial. Forward-looking organizations place a premium on sharing knowledge, developing leaders and teams, fostering creativity, and nurturing professional networks. Leadership experts James O'Toole and Edward Lawler III note that "high-wage, high-profit companies" thrive because they "involve their workers in decision making, reward them fairly for their efforts, and provide them with good training and career opportunities."[18]

In education, on the other hand, teachers and administrators have long mocked much professional development and preparation as unfocused or unhelpful. Public Agenda has found that most teachers with more than 20 years of experience report that professional development has made no difference in their teaching.[19] More than 60 percent of alumni from schools of education report that the schools do not prepare graduates to cope with the realities of today's classrooms. Just one-third of principals think schools of education prepare teachers even moderately well to instruct students with disabilities, diverse cultural backgrounds, or limited English proficiency. Fewer than half of principals say education school graduates are even modestly prepared to use instructional technology, employ performance assessment, or implement curriculum and performance standards.[20]

Finding and cultivating talented employees must be an organization's burning priority. When Larry Bossidy became CEO of global conglomerate Allied Signal in 1991, his executive team evaluated each of the company's 400 managers. Those who met the standard were given additional responsibilities; those who showed promise were coached and evaluated for potential. The rest were counseled out. The company replaced half of its 400 managers within two years. Bossidy explained that finding and developing great leaders is "the job no CEO should delegate."[21]

Trilogy Software, a high-growth technology firm based in Austin, Texas, has created a three-month "boot camp" for new employees, overseen by the company's CEO. During that time employee teams are mentored by veteran executives; develop product ideas, business models, and marketing plans; and take supervised ownership of new projects. At the end of the three months, employees receive comprehensive evaluations based on feedback from colleagues, instructors, and management. These projects have generated more than $100 million in new business, and the company credits the program with fostering camaraderie and boosting motivation among new employees.[22]

At The Container Store, a retail firm that sells storage products, all new hires go through intensive "Foundation Week" training that includes mentoring by high-performing veteran employees. All employees receive at least 235 hours of formal training in their first year (more than 30 times the industry average) and systematically rotate jobs and responsibilities to develop their understanding of the business, develop their customer-service sensibilities, and gain experience that can spark creative problem solving and heightened performance. Employee turnover rates are significantly lower than the industry average.[23] As Gergen and Vanourek have noted, "A container retailer devotes far more time to employee talent development in the first year than does almost any school or district of which we know, even though schools are in the knowledge business."[24]

At Google, employees devote about one day a week to any project that they choose. This policy allows team members to explore new possibilities and creates a pipeline of innovative products and services. In 2006, more than half of Google's new products emerged from this "20 percent rule."[25] Google did not invent this approach; firms including 3M and Intuit have long used versions of it.[26] While there are limits to importing this model into K–12 education, schools or systems might find that variations can be adapted for selected faculty to tackle projects related to troubled student populations, new program design, or community relationships.

The Talent Mind-Set in K–12

Contrast the examples of Trilogy, Google, or even The Container Store with the norm in schooling today. Kaya Henderson has observed that DCPS's teacher evaluation system allows teachers to get a zero for the student-achievement component and still receive an "exceeds expectations" rating.[27] Indeed, school districts frequently seem to operate with the opposite of a talent mind-set. Consider the 2009 search for a new principal for the Houston Independent School District's Mark Twain Elementary School. Twain offers the IB Primary Years Programme. The district ran its "normal" job search that, to the consternation of the school's parent-teacher organization, primarily involved posting the job on the HISD Web site and interviewing internal candidates. Unimpressed, Twain's parents asked the district to expand its search. HISD agreed to post the job on an IB Web site, the National Black Educators Web site, and the National Association of Elementary School Principals Web site. The district then asked Twain's parents to contribute the $800 cost of these heroic, unusual measures—so that other schools would not regard such "extra" recruitment efforts as routine.

Astonishingly, given their mission, schools and districts have long been slapdash when it comes to talent. Jobs are standardized, while performance plays only a marginal role in compensation, job security, or work assignments. State licensure laws set forth the minimum requirements for professional development, and teachers tend to respond by opting for the simplest, least intrusive option on the mediocre menu. Teachers persistently rate most professional development offerings as unhelpful. Meanwhile, most collective bargaining agreements spell out exactly how professional development will be allocated, making it difficult and expensive for districts to provide intensive support to targeted teachers.

It doesn't have to be this way. We can find one intriguing effort to import a talent mind-set into teacher preparation at Teacher U at Hunter College in New York. In 2009, two years after its launch, Teacher U—run by Norman Atkins, former CEO of Uncommon Schools—enrolled 450 teachers in an alternative-certification master's program. Teacher U partners with charter school management organizations KIPP, Uncommon Schools, Achievement First, and the School of Education at Hunter College, CUNY. Tuition support for Teacher U is available from the federal AmeriCorps program, and Teacher U is open to teachers in any New York City charter school, the New York City Teaching Fellows program, and Teach For America corps members. David Steiner, dean of the Hunter College School of Education, explains that key Teacher U program elements include the following:

• The belief that great teaching is taught by prescriptively "focusing on, demonstrating, and practicing the key skills";

• The continuous use of video recordings to provide teachers with feedback and opportunities to reflect on their classroom instruction;

• The requirement that student teachers create detailed lesson plans with explicit "objectives, interactive materials, practice time, and clear assessments" before each session;

• Having instructors evaluate the results of their lessons that same day, using more than 30 indicators; and

• Instituting a master's degree defense that requires student teachers to provide a data-based demonstration of their students' academic progress.

The particulars of just how student performance will be measured and the resulting data utilized are still being refined, but Teacher U makes clear that it is possible to push past stale debates about program design or philosophy when entrepreneurs build on greenfield.

The TEAM Charter Schools in Newark, New Jersey, have developed an apprenticeship program that inducts new teachers and evaluates them on performance. There are at least three key program elements that TEAM founder Ryan Hill has argued "could be fairly easily and inexpensively scaled up." These include (1) assigning apprentice teachers to a master teacher whom they observe and who gives them daily feedback; (2) requiring apprentices to earn their way into a full-class teaching assignment, starting as "coteachers" doing small-group instruction and taking on full classes only after intensive observation and demonstrated performance; and (3) granting mentors a reduced teaching load so that they can provide apprentices daily guidance on planning and instruction.[28] In theory, there is nothing to stop education schools or school districts from emulating the Teacher U or TEAM models. In practice, it turns out to be awfully hard to do this except when building on greenfield.

Ultimately, people are the key to any organization. The goal must not be to simply celebrate best practices but to observe how much time and energy well-run organizations devote to talent and how differently talent can and should be approached in schooling.

Thinking Differently About Talent

Fifty years ago, each teacher would instruct a roomful of students for six hours a day under the savvy management of a principal and would do pretty much this same job for 25 or 30 years. While a lousy way to attract and retain talent, this was a perfectly plausible approach when schools had little competition for the services of smart, college-educated women. Today, this model is no longer tenable, yet the overhang of labor agreements, staffing routines, teacher expectations, and training programs combine to keep it firmly in place.

Schools routinely require all teachers—regardless of skill—to devote roughly equal time and energy to teaching and to bureaucratic duties like patrolling hallways and cafeterias, taking attendance, and compiling report cards. This practice ignores the costs associated with failing to leverage the talent already in schools. For example, some educators are more skilled at teaching reading or mentoring at-risk youth than others, yet schools and school systems operate on the implicit assumption that most teachers will be similarly adept at all of these responsibilities. Two decades of surveys by the National Center for Education Statistics (NCES) suggest that the typical teacher spends only about 68 percent of classroom time on instruction related to core academic subjects, while the remainder is consumed by such activities as administrative tasks, fundraising, assemblies, and socialization. A superior 4th grade reading teacher might teach reading for just 60 or 90 minutes a day but spend five or six hours teaching other subjects, taking lunch and bus duty, and filling out paperwork. Even schools that tout their commitment to professional development and data-driven instruction press teachers to operate as generalists rather than specialists.

Whatever the precise nature of the talent shortage, the reality is that we cannot keep wasting scarce teaching talent. Even Kaya Henderson, the same woman who was able to help conjure 2,500 applicants for the DC Public Schools and is now its hard-charging talent chief, cautions, "There are actually a much smaller number of rock star [teachers] than most people think. And we do not believe that we can build our system on rock star teachers. But we can build a high-performing system on solid performers."[29] Greenfield ventures can pilot strategies that reallocate practitioners to tasks tailored to their talents.

Rewriting the Job Description

The greenfield challenge is to squeeze more juice from the orange by using support staff and technology to allow effective educators to devote more of their time to educating. Schools can do more to systematically assign administrative and other noninstructional tasks to relatively inexpensive support staff, freeing teachers to perform the work for which they are best suited. While K–12 schooling employs a large number of school-based personnel who are not teachers, they are rarely deployed in this fashion. NCES reports that there are more than 600,000 "instructional aides" in K–12 schools, but they are rarely used to maximize teacher effectiveness. Other professions handle specialization and support staff differently. There are 5 million medical professionals in the United States but just 500,000 physicians. The rest are trained practitioners, like nurses, whose complementary talents allow physicians to focus on their specialties.

Attorneys have paralegals and secretaries to do routine paperwork, compile billing reports, or type letters to clients. Some version of this approach, executed thoughtfully and shaped to the needs of particular districts, could allow schools to take greater advantage of faculty strengths and make it easier to address staffing shortages. Alternatively, rather than label personnel simply as teachers, paraprofessionals, or administrative support staff, schools might embrace hybrid positions that allow potential teachers to grow within an organization and leverage and develop their skills in new ways. A district might downsize its central office and invest those dollars in talented veterans who can take on part-time teaching loads and spend the rest of their time on professional development, curriculum development, or parental outreach. Teachers would be able to grow as professionals without abandoning the classroom.

One compelling example is Citizen Schools, which arranges for local volunteers to provide students with highly regarded after-school instruction and career-based learning. Rather than simply mentoring or tutoring students, participants teach weekly modules that tackle complex projects. This leverages the expertise of local professionals who have competing obligations and makes room for valuable part-timers who have a lot to offer. In other fields, organizations tap into particular expertise or retain the service of talented professionals in a variety of ways, including full-time and part-time roles. Such efforts to utilize talent and expertise are rarely evident in schooling.

Tapping into "Citizen Teachers"

Boston-based Citizen Schools was launched in 1995 by founder and CEO Eric Schwarz, with the aim of increasing instructional time, quality, and relevance by providing hands-on learning projects led by local professionals. Today, the program serves 4,400 students on 44 sites.

Schwarz explains how the program's adjunct "Citizen Teachers" can spark student engagement and learning, particularly in the sciences. He observes, "In many of the schools where we partner . . . full-time teachers are now almost entirely focused on basic math and reading instruction because kids are so far behind in these topics. Kids might take science just twice a week, and usually in large classrooms with limited lab facilities and insufficient time to perform experiments or to learn about and apply the scientific method. Citizen Schools recruits chemists and engineers and rocket scientists—literally—and gives kids a chance to take 90-minute classes in the applied sciences, where the kids get to build and launch rockets, design video games, examine cells under a microscope, and otherwise engage in hands-on science."

In a remark that reminds us just how similar the best entrepreneurial and traditional educators are in their motivations and enthusiasms, Schwarz adds, "As the kids get to do science in small learning teams with real scientists, you can literally see the excitement come into their eyes."

Most of the work that Citizen Schools does takes place after school, but the organization has partnered with some schools to offer a longer instructional day (three hours longer) for all kids. In those cases, the school "deputizes" Citizen Schools so that Citizen Teachers lead core instruction in some classes. Some of the early results of these efforts are intriguing. At the Edwards School in Boston, for instance, after two years of the extended school day, 8th graders previously scoring well below the statewide average in math had nearly closed the enormous gap.

"Ultimately Citizen Teachers, particularly in the arts and sciences, could bring a lot to schools, whether they show up to teach at three in the afternoon, as they do now, or at nine in the morning," Schwarz says. "They could coteach with full-time teachers, adding real-world flair and providing a great professional development experience. Or they could lead pull-out classes and apprenticeships, focusing on small groups of kids struggling with traditional instruction or, alternatively, focusing on the highest-performing kids who need an extra challenge."

Technology Replacing Rote Tasks

As discussed in Chapter 4, schools tend to layer new technology atop and around current staffing structures rather than use it to save faculty time or boost productivity. Using new tools to conduct formative assessment can alleviate the need for teachers to devote substantial time to administering tests, calculating grades, and entering data. One such example is Wireless Generation software, which permits early elementary teachers to use Palm Pilots to assess and track early reading performance. Teachers save substantial time in the assessment and data entry process, while faculty and administrators gain immediate access to a wealth of useful performance data. Greenfield ventures should learn from practices like these and rethink ways to reduce staffing requirements while freeing talented educators to do more of the work they do best.

Technology can also change the way services are delivered. Today's educational model assumes a school with many classrooms, each featuring a teacher working alone with a group of 25 students. This strategy is familiar but expensive, and it fails to take advantage of the technology that has revolutionized other sectors. For instance, Web-based instruction wipes away the barriers posed by distance and means that a teacher with whiteboard technology can work one-on-one with a student thousands of miles away almost as easily as with one in the same room.

Perhaps the most significant impact of education technology is its potential to eliminate obstacles that geography poses. Web-based delivery systems can take advantage of the wealth of highly educated, English-speaking people in nations like India who are willing to tutor children at relatively inexpensive rates. Washington, DC–based SMARTHINKING Inc. uses American and international tutors to provide intensive tutoring to students. Students can log onto the company's Web site 24 hours a day, 7 days a week, and work in real time with experts in various academic subjects. Technology can also make it easier for schools to enlist educators who may be unwilling to relocate, for schools in different locations to communicate or share staff, and for central administrators to deliver support to campuses hundreds of miles away.

Some skeptics have suggested that technology cannot be substituted for, or meaningfully augment, the work that teachers do. This point of view largely explains education's failure to exploit new technologies—from the television to the PC to the Internet—as labor-saving devices. Instead, schools have floundered under a "supplement, not supplant" approach in which computers collect dust in the back of classrooms for all but 30 or 60 minutes a day, and educators teach pretty much the same way they always have. Too often, discussions about the use of digital tools, Web-based delivery, and instructional software fail to consider how staffing must change before schools can realize technology's potential.

Rethinking Pay

Rethinking recruitment assumptions and job descriptions includes a wholly new model for salaries and benefits. Today, even proponents of compensation reform mostly just advocate paying more to teachers who raise student test scores, complete additional training, or achieve National Board Certification. Even under most merit pay plans, starting teachers begin at roughly the same salary with similar job descriptions and proceed along a relatively standard-ized career ladder. This would be akin to law firms requiring every new JD to start as a paralegal and then become a lawyer, or hospitals requiring every new MD to begin as a nurse and then become a general practitioner, and then a specialist—with each role linked to predetermined, rigid pay scales.

Law and medicine have largely severed the formal link between organi-zational hierarchy and compensation. By allowing pay to reflect value rather than seniority or titles, these fields allow accomplished attorneys or doctors to be rewarded according to exceptional skills and performance. We need green-field models that import this kind of thinking to teaching. It is not enough to stack bonuses atop industrial-era pay scales. Where teachers take on new roles, compensation should be rethought accordingly. If teachers are tutoring over the Internet, for example, employers will need radically different pay-ment strategies to recruit, reward, and retain talented instructors.

Welcoming Entrepreneurs

The unmanageability of school systems, the lack of rewards and recognition for excellence, the paucity of venture funding, limited autonomy, a bias in favor of people who have "come up through the system," and a culture averse to risk taking all make K–12 schooling inhospitable to entrepreneurs. Attract-ing entrepreneurial talent begins by taking these barriers head on.

One man who knows a bit about what entrepreneurial leadership requires is Steve Jobs, cofounder and CEO of Apple Inc., who oversaw the launch of such modest successes as the iPod, the iPhone, and iTunes. In 2007, at a school reform conclave in Texas, Jobs opined, "What's wrong with our schools in this nation is that they have become unionized in the worst possible way. . . . What kind of person could you get to run a small business if you told them that, when they came in, they couldn't get rid of people that they thought weren't any good?"[30]

Most educational leaders have had little exposure to entrepreneurial skill sets. Indeed, today's education leadership preparation fails to provide even the most basic tools, let alone an entrepreneurial toolkit. Public Agenda has reported that 96 percent of principals say that their colleagues were more helpful than their graduate studies in preparing them for the job, and two-thirds say that "leadership programs in graduate schools of education are out of touch."[31] Arthur Levine, former president of Teachers College, has concluded that "the majority of [educational administration] programs range from inadequate to appalling."[32] As we noted in Chapter 3, the socialization and training of today's leaders focus exclusively on equipping them to oversee traditional operations rather than to launch or grow new ones.

Vibrant entrepreneurial sectors are marked by formal and informal mechanisms that enable people to meet, share ideas and lessons, find opportunities for career advancement, and learn about new developments. One such example is Teach for America's summer leadership institute for corps members. Consider that in 2008, TFA received nearly 25,000 applications and accepted just 3,700 individuals (15 percent).[33] Indeed, TFA is one of the most popular organizations to work for among college seniors. Sixteen percent of Spelman College seniors applied to TFA in 2008, as did 11 percent of seniors at Morehouse, Williams, and Yale and 10 percent of seniors from Duke, Georgetown, the University of Chicago, Wake Forest, and Wesleyan.[34] Among the ranks of TFA alumni are entrepreneurs like Mike Feinberg and David Levin, who founded the KIPP Academies; Michelle Rhee, who founded The New Teacher Project and is now the chancellor of the District of Columbia Public Schools; and Kim Smith, who founded the NewSchools Venture Fund.[35]

More broadly, TFA serves as a magnet and natural network for entrepreneurial personalities. The networking is particularly powerful because, contrary to some public perceptions, two-thirds of TFA corps members remain involved in education after completing their initial two-year commitment.[36] TFA works to keep alumni connected to its network with a career center that provides professional guides, alumni mentors, and a job-posting board. Eighteen regional staff members arrange opportunities for alumni to network in locales across the country, while TFA hosts annual summits that foster alumni connections, expose them to national and community leaders, and help them explore career opportunities. TFA also publishes the magazine *One Day*, which is distributed to 20,000 subscribers throughout the year.

For Education Pioneers, a national human capital organization that recruits and trains individuals who are enrolled in or have just completed graduate school, networking is a core part of its mission. According to Sheryl

Linsky, Education Pioneers' director of alumni engagement, in 2009, Education Pioneers received 1,750 applicants for 225 spots. The 2009 applicants included 510 education school students, 492 business school students, and 312 law school students. Applicants disproportionately come from highly selective institutions; the 2009 applicant pool, for example, included 106 students from the Harvard Graduate School of Education. Applicants average more than four years of work experience and an undergraduate GPA of 3.5.

Education Pioneers helps its fellows apply their training and skills to schooling by pairing them with an organization (partners include Teach for America, KIPP, and Green Dot Public Schools) for a 10-week summer fellowship. Two-thirds of Education Pioneers fellows pursue positions in education after graduation.[37]

Education Pioneers is also beginning to place an emphasis on maintaining connections with its alumni through career assistance, an online community, and continued professional development. Linsky explains that the organization has a career center with job postings and a contact-information database to help alumni get connected. It has also developed an online community and hosts events to facilitate career support as well as provide additional opportunities for professional development. She adds, "We do events throughout the year, which are meant to be networking events as well as career-supporting events. . . . We're helping alumni find that first full-time job in education and then supporting them in professional development." She also notes that Education Pioneers provides professional development services even to alumni who do not work in education, anticipating that they are more likely to return to the sector if the connection is maintained.

Avoiding the Pitfalls of Greenfield Success

Monica Higgins, a professor at the Harvard Graduate School of Education and the author of *Career Imprints*, has explained that entrepreneurial organizations face common pitfalls when it comes to recruiting and training talent. Today, many of the elite greenfield organizations rely upon a "mitosis" approach in which they largely limit growth to "pods" spun off by individuals steeped in the organization's culture. This clannish model has strengths but also serious limitations.

First, it leaves organizations dependent on their ability to find talented, high-energy members ready and willing to launch new pods. If the well is shallow, or if these individuals burn out, this strategy becomes self-limiting. Second, mitosis dramatically limits the speed at which organizations can expand. Third, mitosis is a fragile model for growth: It presumes that organizations can and should keep doing what they have done before, the same way they have done it, and that clones will prove similarly effective everywhere.

One reason that clanlike models initially "work" is their uniform approach to what Higgins has termed an "organizational career imprint"—instilling a set of capabilities, connections, confidence, and cognitions that individuals share. The result is a kind of organizational DNA that helps ventures thrive in the short term but may ultimately hinder their ability to adapt, evolve, and grow.

Giving new hires extremely challenging work assignments—"stretch assignments"—when they join an organization is central to imprinting. The upside is that individuals enjoy a tremendous sense of empowerment and self-efficacy early on, and leadership becomes truly shared. Yet there are also downsides to stretch assignments. In particular, those doing the stretching may become overwhelmed or exhausted.

Organizations can also strengthen imprinting by providing social reinforcement throughout employee training and development. Hiring in cohorts or seeing that peers experience similar developmental paths can instill shared norms and expectations. These strong networks foster commitment and collaboration, clarify organizational identity, and facilitate role-modeling and mentoring. One potential downside is inbreeding and inadvertently developing blind spots.

A third factor that strengthens imprinting is demonstrated success. When individuals see that organizational routines "work," they are more likely to repeat them faithfully. Showcasing successes can also attract new waves of talent and funding. But early "success" can also be perilous, leaving organizations insulated and self-congratulatory—and short-circuiting thoughtful reflection on what needs to be improved. The same factors that help deliver early success can become flaws if unchecked. Savvy operators address these challenges not by shying from a strong culture but by tempering it sensibly. To counter excessive groupthink, it is important to seek alternative pools of talent and build relationships that offer fresh perspectives and thinking. The aim for greenfielders is not producing cookie-cutter models or true believers, but models and employees able to adapt to varied locales, clienteles, and challenges.[38]

Filling the Talent Pipeline in New Orleans

The talent question requires both policy changes and practical action. By now, it should come as no surprise that Matt Candler has been in a position to offer a firsthand account of what it means to tackle the talent pipeline. When we left Candler in Chapter 4, he was fighting to ensure quality control in New York charter schooling. Here, he shares an experience from his next position: CEO of New Schools for New Orleans (NSNO), a role in which he struggled to help rebuild schools in New Orleans after Hurricane Katrina. A few days after the levees broke in August 2005, Louisiana took over every New Orleans school that was below the state average, or 107 of 125 schools: "Suddenly, the state bureaucracy designed to oversee all local districts was in charge of a 60,000-student system."[39]

Sarah Usdin, the former executive director of both Teach For America and The New Teacher Project in New Orleans, launched NSNO in 2006 and recruited Candler to leave New York and take the post of CEO that year. NSNO's mission was threefold: attracting and preparing talent to teach and lead, launching and supporting open-enrollment public charter schools, and advocating for accountable and sustainable high-quality public schools.

Having just left New York City, Candler recalls that the biggest difference between the Big Apple and the Big Easy was how much easier it was to get people to move to, and stay in, New York than post-Katrina New Orleans. Even with all the publicity that had turned New Orleans into a hot place for young do-gooders, the longstanding culture of low expectations and the lack of New York's energetic appeal made it more difficult to attract talent. And, Candler observed, it is the talent equation that "will make or break us." To move forward on building the pipeline of teacher and principal talent, NSNO reached out to partners such as The New Teacher Project and New Leaders for New Schools and took steps to help make their models work under especially chaotic circumstances. NSNO functioned as "a one-stop shop" to help the programs avoid the fragmentation inherent in serving dozens of stand-alone schools and especially exacerbated in New Orleans, where half of the local schools were charters. NSNO also managed to lower costs for each provider by giving free office space and subsidizing a portion of staff costs.

In addition to recruiting teachers and principals, NSNO moved to tackle other talent challenges that greenfielders rarely address. One such initiative was recruiting and training charter school board members, an important role that rarely receives serious attention. Candler explains, "Charter school leadership is not just about school principals. With half of the schools in the city operating as charters, the sudden need for strong board members is acute. Boards, not school leaders, have legal accountability for school performance. In addition to training existing boards and those still in the startup process, we actively recruit and orient future board members. . . . We host 'speed-dating' sessions and citywide orientations designed to match potential board members with schools."

Candler points to NSNO's program for nurturing new schools as an obvious example of how greenfielders can boost the likelihood that new schools will have the leaders they need. He notes, "Our School Incubation Program, a 12- to 14-month residency-based training program that prepares promising educators to open their own charter schools, is designed to recruit talent from the rest of the country and to train bench players in the strongest local schools to speed replication efforts. . . . Ours is, for now, positioned to train more new founders than successors in existing schools. Growing local school leaders is a riskier strategy that may not be required in New York, but it is likely to be necessary [in most other locales]."[40]

Conclusion

When it comes to enhancing talent in K–12 education, there are three distinct challenges: doing a better job of recruiting and developing talent, finding ways to staff schools and use technology to get more value from the talent we have, and then surfacing and supporting potential entrepreneurs.

Charter management organizations like Achievement First and Uncommon Schools have done an impressive job of attracting talent and finding passionate educators. The question is how far their strategies will go. NewSchools Venture Fund founder Kim Smith has noted, "The KIPP model works as long as you have really exceptional leaders to replicate the network's high quality. Over time, they will be more difficult to find."[41]

It is essential to recruit and better develop the talent pool. This means competing for 21st century college graduates and leveraging the strategies used in other fields to recruit from other sectors. This entails pioneering staffing models and harnessing technology in ways that allow educators to more effectively serve children, more fully exploit instructional tools, and wrestle with questions of school and system design. One important part of this is developing hybrid positions that allow teachers to remain in the classrooms while building skill sets and gaining experience in other contexts.

Cultivating a greenfield talent pool also means erecting the scaffolding that enables enterprising individuals to recruit talented team members, collaborate with mentors, discover business opportunities, and share information. Entities like Teach For America and KIPP now boast sizable alumni networks, and annual gatherings have served to keep their members and alumni connected with each other, with funders, and with other potential supporters. Those who are interested in creating greenfield must nurture and expand these kinds of networks. We'll have more to say on this count in the next chapter.

Promising initiatives like New Leaders for New Schools or The New Teacher Project are aiming to improve the flow of talent into K–12 education *in spite of* the considerable policy barriers that currently exist, and to create a system that works in concert with talent providers rather than against them. The goal cannot be some best practice, jargon-laden, "human capital" fix; instead, it should be to allow schools and providers to experiment and constantly learn from one another. None of this, however, will amount to much without resources. It is to that challenge that we now turn.

6

MONEY

NEW VENTURES can neither launch nor grow without money. In the absence of funding, greenfield efforts become soul-sucking endeavors for their founders, proceed much more slowly than necessary, or never get off the ground at all. The famous KIPP Academies almost died before seeing the light of day because founders Mike Feinberg and David Levin had trouble assembling the few thousand dollars they needed to get started. Raising those funds required the two to write scores of letters and make countless appeals to Houston-area donors. As *Washington Post* reporter Jay Mathews has wryly recounted in his colorful history of KIPP, *Work Hard, Be Nice*, "Out of more than one hundred letters, only about a third responded. Most said, in polite corporate language, that they had never heard of KIPP and didn't like the sound of it. None promised money."[1]

Teach For America's Wendy Kopp also struggled to find funding when launching TFA. She has described being schooled by Princeton faculty in just how hard it would be to raise the requisite funds, remembering, "What [Professor Bressler] really wanted to know, he said in his booming voice, was how in the world I planned to raise the $2.5 million. . . . He didn't seem convinced. 'Do you know how hard it is to raise twenty-five *hundred* dollars?' he asked."[2]

Kopp has described sitting down with Texas billionaire and former presidential candidate Ross Perot, trying to get that $2.5 million:

> All I remember is Mr. Perot talking. He talked a lot, and I had trouble following much of what he was saying. I was mostly just thinking "I need to

stay here until I get $1 million from this man." When Mr. Perot suggested that I contact Sam Walton and other philanthropists instead, I insisted that he himself was the best possible prospect. Finally, after two hours of back and forth, Mr. Perot agreed to offer us a challenge grant of $500,000. We would have to match his money three to one. I'm not sure what ultimately led Mr. Perot to this idea. He must have realized that I wasn't planning to go anywhere until he committed to something.[3]

Kopp remembers that Perot's grant was "the catalyst we needed," with other donors following his lead and supplying the remaining funds "in relatively short order."

Only the most hard-headed or selfless of entrepreneurs muscle through. Those with less stomach for frustration, as well as those interested in doing well in addition to doing good, will steer their energies elsewhere. It's not just about dollars, though. The impact of venture capital in entrepreneurial hotbeds like Silicon Valley is also a product of the personal networks, mentoring, and expertise that come with it. These networks help new enterprises get a foot in the door, and mentors provide assistance with mundane, but crucial, tasks like organizational bookkeeping, strategic planning, and governance.

Equally crucial is the quality control implicit in venture funding. Those who worry that greenfield efforts may not be publicly run, or who are hesitant to give funds to new ventures with unproven quality, often overlook the fact that competition for venture funding in the private sector comes with intensive screening. In a community like Silicon Valley, as a general rule, only 10 percent of business plans that venture capitalists receive warrant any response at all, and only 1 percent are ever funded. To be sure, venture investment also has its share of blemishes. During the late-1990s dot-com bubble, for instance, investors frequently left their skepticism behind as they flocked to a slew of dubious ventures. So it is not that this process is flawless, but only that it tends to exert a healthy discipline overall.

A particular challenge for schooling is that venture capital is not geographically dispersed. While schools operate in every corner of the country, venture capital is highly concentrated. In 2006, one-third of all venture capital investments were made in California's Silicon Valley. That figure increases to about half of all investments if Los Angeles, Orange County, and San Diego are included and to three-fourths of all U.S. venture investment if one adds the Route 128 corridor outside Boston, New York, and metropolitan Washington,

DC.[4] In other words, about three-fourths of all investment is made in a few California locales and in the Boston–New York–Washington nexus. Given this natural dynamic, we cannot expect 15,000 school districts to become hotbeds of educational entrepreneurship. Instead, the expectation should be that the requisite funding, infrastructure, and networks will likely emerge in some limited number of locales. Greenfielders need to invest in and build these hubs, and then take care to encourage and support the ventures that are able and willing to deliver their services more broadly.

The quality control and support that the investment process provides are driven by investors tending to their self-interest and happen naturally and invisibly in places like Silicon Valley. They impose a certain flexible but hardnosed quality control even while creating an entire ecosystem and equipping promising new ventures to take root. For too long, these quality-assurance and development processes have been overlooked by K–12 reformers who wonder why innovations fizzle, and by school choice enthusiasts who seemingly expect tidy rows of flowers to spring from a barren, rubble-strewn plain.

What Is Venture Capital?

Crucial money for greenfield ventures is startup funding—the kind of investments that are often referred to in business magazines or popular culture as "venture capital." Venture capital plays a key role in launching and supporting the firms responsible for innovation and growth in the U.S. economy.

Companies backed by venture capital include many of today's titans, like Intel, Microsoft, Medtronic, Apple, Google, Genentech, Starbucks, Whole Foods, and eBay.[5] In 2007 and 2008, the National Venture Capital Association reports that there were more than 2,400 venture capital deals worth more than $13 billion in the United States, with the bulk of activity concentrated in knowledge-driven industries like software, biotechnology, medical devices, and energy.[6] One would normally expect to see education comfortably ensconced on a list like that—yet it is nowhere in sight.

Since such funding is largely alien to most individuals involved in K–12 education, it is worth taking a moment to understand how venture capital typically works. What exactly is a venture capital fund? It is typically an investment fund initiated by a group of partners who contribute their own money and then raise additional dollars from outside investors. The partnership agreement specifies both the life span of the fund (typically 10 years) and the management fee. As Joe Keeney and Daniel Pianko have explained, "The typical management fee structure is 'two and twenty'—that is, 2 percent per year of the total capital raised, plus 20 percent of the profits after . . . 100 percent of their invested capital [has been recovered] at the end of the fund's life."[7] Over those 10 years, venture firms raise funds, pursue promising investments, and eventually exit by selling their stake.

Given the risks, venture capital investors seek to win big or cut their losses. For this reason, they typically provide only enough funding for a venture to reach the next stage of development so that it can attract support from those with a smaller tolerance for risk. This need to realize investment returns leads new ventures to focus on becoming successful enough to attract buyers, which involves a private transaction or "going public" and selling shares of stock. And a venture capitalist's aim—to win big on the front end and get out fast once the profit is made—leads venture firms to identify an exit strategy early on.

The Three Phases of Investment

Though all educational entrepreneurs need financing to get off the ground (*venture capital*) and to support expansion (*growth capital*), the capital market for for-profit organizations is markedly different from the one that nonprofit organizations can access. (See Figure 6.1.) While for-profit ventures can theoretically rely on their profits, nonprofits rely on a continuous funding stream (*sustaining capital*) even after they mature.

Startup Capital

Education entrepreneurs creating for-profit enterprises traditionally raise their initial capital from individuals ("angel investors") or venture capital firms.

Figure 6.1
Types of Financial Support Needed

	Start-Up	Growth	Sustaining
For-profit	Equity investments from venture capital firms or "angel investors"	Equity investments from later-stage venture capital firms	Revenue from product or services
Nonprofit	Grants from individual donors, foundations, and public sources	Grants from foundations and public sources Program-related investments (loans from foundations)	Continued fundraising for grants Revenue from sales of product or service

Source: Kim Smith and Julie Landry Petersen, Figure 2 (Types of Financial Support Needed), "What is Educational Entrepreneurship?" from *Educational Entrepreneurship: Realities, Challenges, Possibilities,* edited by Frederick M. Hess (Cambridge, MA: Harvard Education Press, 2006), p. 35. For more information, please visit www.harvardeducationpress.org, or call 1-888-437-1437.

As explained, these investors put up cash in exchange for an ownership stake ("equity") in the new organization, and they expect that their investment will eventually yield a profit.

In 2004, just over $50 million was privately invested in businesses address-ing the Pre-K–12 sector.[8] With success stories like Amazon, Apple, and Google, one might think that early venture investors typically do quite well for themselves. But the reality is much more complex. In the book *Fool's Gold*, Scott Shane, a professor of entrepreneurial studies at Case Western Reserve University, argues that observers focus on fabulously successful entrepre-neurs, but what they do not realize is that these success stories are incredibly rare. Only a small number of entrepreneurs are really, really successful—and, by extension, only a small number of venture investors see large returns. The media contributes to this misperception because it is easy to tell the story of Google and of early Google investors, but it is much less interesting and more difficult to write stories about failure.[9]

Nonprofit educational entrepreneurs generally raise their startup capi-tal from venture philanthropy firms like NewSchools Venture Fund and the Charter School Growth Fund, or from individual donors and foundations. Only a few foundations are comfortable taking a risk on entrepreneurial education organizations. Those that do make these early funds available— usually via multimillion-dollar grants over the course of several years—tend to be younger foundations, like the Eli and Edythe Broad Foundation, the Milton Friedman Foundation, the Michael and Susan Dell Foundation, and the Bill & Melinda Gates Foundation, that have embraced the modern school of venture philanthropy.

Before the relatively recent emergence of these new foundations, funders tended to provide these early grants in only small increments, forcing entre-preneurs to spend enormous amounts of time and energy on fundraising from multiple donors. In addition, foundation officials found it far more palatable to support a host of small, capacity-building grants than to make concen-trated bets on greenfield ventures. Foundation officials rarely get in trouble for failing to have an impact, but can quickly get into hot water for supporting politically contentious measures. For this reason, traditional funders have his-torically preferred to support professional development, curricular reforms, mentoring programs, and similar efforts that are broadly popular and appear to be risk-free.

Scrambling for Startup Capital

Eric Adler is cofounder and managing director of the SEED Foundation, a grades 7–12 boarding school in Washington, DC, that has won awards from Harvard University's Kennedy School of Government and other entities for its astonishing success sending at-risk kids to college. Adler relates how he and cofounder Rajiv Vinnakota struggled to find funding for the initial DC boarding school. At first, Adler explains, "We thought we were going to build a private school."

After a quick analysis of boarding program costs and research into what it would require in terms of annual funding or raising an endowment, however, Adler and his partner concluded that "it was not economically feasible. We would have been talking about many hundreds of millions of dollars of endowment. Or it would have meant raising money hand-to-mouth year after year." Instead, Adler and Vinnakota began looking at nonprofit models in which the government might provide startup capital and then SEED would raise money annually to sustain the school. "You get the slug up front because everyone needs some activation energy and some capital to get going, and then after that you raise the money year after year," Adler explains. But, he adds, "we . . . pretty quickly concluded that that wasn't going to work, either. Because, again, it was going to involve a level of annual fundraising that just wasn't sustainable."

After dismissing those two strategies, Adler wondered, "Could [we] reverse it? Could [we] go to the private sector and get the upfront slug of money in exchange for getting the public sector to promise the operating costs indefinitely?" This led the SEED Foundation to charter schooling. Adler recalls Vinnakota and himself approaching DC and federal officials and saying, "In exchange for the private sector putting up a whole bunch of new facility money, would you be willing, then, to pay the difference between the regular day cost and the boarding cost?" And they were talking simultaneously to philanthropists and private-sector investors, saying, "Yes, we need to raise a bunch of money from you now, and we'll still have to raise some in the first few years while we're getting up to scale. But once we get up to scale, we promise we'll never come back to you saying we won't survive unless [you're willing to provide additional support]." This strategy allowed the SEED Foundation to raise the required $25 million for the 1999–2003 launch of the school.

Growth Capital

For an educational entrepreneur, finding startup capital is challenging, but fundraising for growth can be even tougher. For-profit companies that have a good track record may find that venture capital firms such as Quad Ventures are willing to invest in growth for later-stage education organizations with promising early results. Even venture capital firms that don't focus on education are willing to entertain the notion if they see a successful business emerging.

Nonprofits, on the other hand, have a much more difficult time attracting growth funds. They struggle to raise the kind of large, multiyear investments needed to support expansion because even terrific nonprofit ventures cannot deliver a handsome return to investors. In addition, there is a perverse incentive for growing nonprofit organizations: The better the organization is doing, the more likely donors are to drop their support, believing they have done their part or are no longer needed. As such, many foundations seem willing to support strong nonprofit organizations and help them expand on a limited scale, but few are willing to sustain an organization as it grows over time.

It is especially difficult to raise large amounts of funding from foundations because, according to federal regulations, program officers need only spend 5 percent of the foundation's total assets each year in the form of grants and other expenses. Except in unusual cases, the other 95 percent of a foundation's assets are not used to fund grantees but instead are invested for the long term to preserve its endowment. If foundations are to seek a bigger impact, they may need to tap these endowments more aggressively.

One strategy for augmenting the available funding relies on *program-related investments*, which are loans that come from endowment funds. Several foundations, including the Walton Family Foundation and the Annie E. Casey Foundation, have made program-related investments to help charter school entrepreneurs secure facilities for their schools. There is room for more such investment: According to the Foundation Center, foundations nationwide hold nearly $500 billion in their endowments but use just over $200 million of that for charitable loans or program-related investments—less than one-twentieth of 1 percent.[10]

Nonprofits and philanthropies that have taken on the explicit mission of helping other nonprofits grow include the Growth Philanthropy Network, the Draper Richards Foundation, the Robin Hood Foundation, and the Tipping Point Foundation. The Draper Richards Foundation, for instance, was founded by famed venture capitalist Bill Draper and seeks to give nonprofits both management knowledge (a Draper Richards board member sits on participating nonprofits' boards) and capital in their infant stages ($100,000 per year for three years).

Another foundation that is doing things differently is SeaChange Capital Partners, which makes multimillion-dollar infusions to help established nonprofits grow. SeaChange was founded by Chuck Harris, a retired Goldman Sachs partner. Harris had previously worked with nonprofit organizations and noted a serious problem. He explains:

> I was involved with a couple of nonprofit organizations that had fantastic management, good results, a fair amount of financial discipline, and were ambitious. And if they had been for-profit businesses at a similar stage of development, they would have gone out and raised a multimillion-dollar, multiyear round of funding tied to their business plan. Instead, they were sending out scattershot proposals for relatively small amounts of money over short periods of time. In other words, there was no financial certainty . . . [and] the most senior people in the organization were spending a disproportionate amount of their time fundraising as opposed to driving the ship. It seemed to me to be a very ad hoc, inefficient, and restrictive way to grow.[11]

SeaChange adopts Wall Street methods to support proven nonprofits with ambitious growth plans. Harris explains the key shift is "seek[ing] to fund the business plans of these nonprofits rather than [to] fund a piece of their program. . . . We plan to conduct the financing much like a private placement in the business sector, with the goal of raising $5 million, $10 million, $15 million for organizations on the threshold of a growth phase."[12]

Sustaining Capital

Entrepreneurial K–12 ventures launch and grow with private capital or philanthropic support. Once up and running, however, sustainable ventures seek to rely on earned income from fees or the sale of products or services. However, despite increasing acceptance of income-generating for-profit and nonprofit organizations, few educational entrepreneurs have built models that sustain themselves on these revenues alone. And, as Dan Katzir and Wendy Hassett of the Eli & Edythe Broad Foundation have observed, "Many foundations will not support a grantee for more than a specified number of years, regardless of where the organization is in terms of its growth cycle."[13] This means that nonprofits scramble to find ways to offset the loss of philanthropic support by finding ways to sell their services or by finding new funders, while for-profits seek to achieve a scale that makes them economically viable. One of the few successful school builders to have addressed this challenge is the National Heritage Academies (NHA), a for-profit charter operator that enrolls 35,000 students in

57 schools across six states and has managed to attain profitability while generating impressive academic outcomes. Even academically successful ventures, however, have found it challenging to mimic NHA's financial success.

Although some nonprofit educational entrepreneurs can support their organization's ongoing operations through public funding—such as by per-pupil dollars that flow to charter management organizations—most rely, at least in part, on fundraising from individuals and foundations.

The Three Sources of Capital

In education, there are three sources that might support new or expanding greenfield ventures: public revenues, philanthropies, and profit-seeking investors. Historically, profit-seeking dollars have driven the entrepreneurial engine in most sectors. In K–12 schooling, on the other hand, aside from a burst of interest in educational management organizations during the mid-1990s, such investment has been rare.

Public Revenues

Public spending dominates the K–12 sector. State, local, and federal governments spent over $500 billion in 2005 on K–12 schooling—about 90 percent of all money expended on public and private schools. The federal government provides funding streams to states and districts; states and localities fund school systems; and the expenditures wind up almost entirely driven by state or district officials. But the vast majority of this spending is dedicated to salaries, benefits, school operations, and other routine line items. Vanishingly little is available for research, development, or new ventures. In fact, researchers have calculated that up to 70 percent of district money is formulaically allocated as soon as it arrives in the central office and never even appears in school budgets.[14] As University of Washington professor Paul Hill has concluded, "Public school systems can be fully open to entrepreneurship only if money that is now tied up can be released and reallocated."[15]

Outside of the limited funding it provides for charter school facilities, the government channels little funding to entrepreneurial ventures. One such program that does exist is the U.S. Department of Education's Credit Enhancement for Charter School Facilities program, which provides several million dollars in grants intended to boost the credit of charter schools so that they can tap into private-sector capital to acquire, construct, renovate, or lease facilities.[16] Another is the State Charter School Facilities Incentive Grants Program, which provides about $10 million to $15 million a year in grants to help fund programs that provide charter school facilities.[17]

The problem is that even when elected officials think it a good idea to revamp spending, political costs can seem prohibitive. One school builder I spoke with recalls a conversation he had with a governor while pursuing state funds:

> [The governor told me,] "I don't have a doubt that what you're talking about works. And furthermore, I don't have a doubt that in the long run, the taxpayer is better off for making this investment. But here I am [a Democratic governor with a Republican legislature], and I'm going to have to pay an enormous political cost to generate the revenues required to pay for the program. . . . And the Republicans in the legislature will make sure that I pay an exorbitant political cost for producing those revenues so that some governor two or three or four governors from now can reap the benefits [of the program's success]. I don't have a political equation that works like that."

Given that public spending dominates K–12 schooling, successful ventures must be able to compete for those dollars if they are to ever achieve substantial scale. The logic is straightforward: With philanthropies contributing perhaps $3 billion a year to K–12 education, and taxpayers providing more than $500 billion, it is not feasible for new ventures to thrive otherwise. New Leaders for New Schools cofounder Jon Schnur has observed that funding systems "do not reward things that are working. . . . Right now, organizations have to demonstrate additional inputs in order to get additional funding. What if we were to say, instead, 'You are getting results and serving more kids and serving kids better, and therefore you get more funding'?"[18]

An intriguing attempt to do this was included in the 2009 American Recovery and Reinvestment Act (ARRA), which set aside $5 billion in public funds to support innovation by states, districts, and nontraditional providers. How these dollars are allocated and used will be instructive. The worry is that such a centralized pool of national funds yields at least two obvious problems. One is the temptation to fund familiar, politically palatable, "more, better" ventures, even if they are boutiques that are costly or likely to prove difficult to grow. The other is the risk that political considerations and personal connections will drive funding. Early signs in the ARRA application criteria offer some cause for concern, suggesting a tendency to think as engineers, rather than gardeners. Ultimately, a more promising strategy may rely upon smaller, less centralized approaches to public investment, such as that modeled by the Vermont Sustainable Jobs Fund (VSJF).

The Vermont Sustainable Jobs Fund was established in 1995 by the state legislature as a nonprofit, public-private 501(c)3 organization to invest in market-based solutions to environmental challenges. It offers grants and technical assistance to Vermont entrepreneurs with promising business models in sustainable agriculture, forestry, and renewable energy. From 1997 to 2006, the VSJF received more than $2 million in state funds and leveraged an additional $4.7 million from other state, federal, and philanthropic sources. By coordinating funding and nonfinancial support, it seeks to help the ventures it supports survive their initial phases until they are able to tap private investment. "The opportunity for us is that we get to try riskier propositions," says VSJF executive director Ellen Kahler. "We get to take chances that state entities like the Department of Economic Development just can't. We think of ourselves as pioneers."[19]

Philanthropy

In the absence of dedicated public financing, educational entrepreneurs have typically relied heavily on philanthropic support. The limits to this approach are legion, however, as scholars estimate that total philanthropy to K–12 education probably amounts to less than $3 billion a year—or less than 1 percent of all K–12 spending.[20] To date, entrepreneurial ventures have been disproportionately funded by this tiny sliver of funding—and especially by funds from younger foundations with roots in the 21st century economy.

Some leading "new" philanthropies, like the Gates, Walton, and Broad foundations, have attempted to adopt the venture investment mind-set to the social sector. Funders have begun to weigh criteria like scalability and financial sustainability more heavily, have taken seats on nonprofit boards, and have requested regular performance updates. This marks a shift in thinking—though it's a development that has also encountered skepticism as to how willing these funders actually are to take bold chances and whether their efforts sometimes cross from smart oversight into micromanagement. Whatever one makes of such concerns, it is clear that support from philanthropic funders has proven instrumental in launching or expanding heralded greenfield ventures like KIPP, New Leaders for New Schools, Aspire Public Schools, College Summit, Green Dot, and Achievement First.

Despite this shift, the philanthropic market for educational entrepreneurs lacks many of the elements that make for success in the capital markets of other industries, such as clear definition of success and good performance information. Given the dearth of good data on providers, and the near-absence of data on cost-effectiveness, funders have limited information available when making investment decisions. As a result, donors are frequently tempted to spread their available funds thinly among multiple ventures, embrace outsized personalities, jump on the bandwagon of the latest fad, or rely too heavily on people they happen to know and schools they have seen. As one funder told me, "In the absence of good-quality data, relationships matter too much." All of this adds up to investments that do less than they might to seed greenfield.

In education circles, the two best-known venture philanthropies may be the decade-old NewSchools Venture Fund and the much younger Charter School Growth Fund. The San Francisco–based NewSchools Venture Fund secures investments from both for-profit and nonprofit sources and then seeks to provide startup capital to ventures—both nonprofit and for-profit organizations—that are sustainable and designed to achieve scale. The Colorado-based Charter School Growth Fund, with over $150 million in support, provides grants and loans to promote the growth of high-quality charter management and support organizations. These venture philanthropists accept that some investments will fail, so long as the failures are the product of efforts to address hard, important challenges. As the Broad Foundation's Katzir and Hassett have explained, "We do not regard our grant-making as charity . . . [but] think of our work as making investments in areas in which we expect a healthy return."[21]

Another investment model that is linked to traditional districts is that of the $15 million Chicago Public Education Fund (CPEF), overseen by founding president Janet Knupp and charged with funding "well-managed, high-impact programs that improve school leadership and student achievement system-wide." CPEF and similar district funds like the Fund for Public Schools in

New York City and New Jersey's Newark Charter School Fund operate as investment funds and partner with a particular school district. CPEF's first investment fund totaled $10 million, and the second $15 million—small figures compared to the $5 billion Chicago Public Schools budget, but amounts that have had a surprisingly sizable impact. Knupp explains, "Our investments extend far beyond financial capital. We provide strategic management and operational assistance including taking board seats [in the providers that CPEF invests in], hiring management teams, crafting strategic business plans, and identifying key outcomes that are tied to the infusion of dollars. Perhaps most importantly, we ensure on the front end that there is a viable exit strategy. Ultimately, we expect our programs to become part and parcel of how the district does business."[22] There are a variety of models deserving exploration, each with its own strengths.

For-Profit Investment

Tapping new dollars beyond those available from government or philanthropists requires attracting private capital. As Tom Vander Ark, the first executive director of education for the Bill & Melinda Gates Foundation and now managing partner with Revolution Learning, has noted, "Private capital is particularly useful in producing and scaling innovative products and services. . . . In an efficient market, money flows to good ideas. The inefficiency of the U.S. K–12 education sector has hampered investment and innovation."[23]

That said, it's important we not romanticize the wisdom or foresight of investors any more than we do that of government officials or philanthropists. In education, investors have at times been guilty of wishful thinking, herd behavior, and failing to understand American education before diving into it. Mike Sandler, founder of Eduventures, a Boston-based market research firm that covers the education industry, notes, "After the Internet bubble burst, venture capitalists reinvented themselves as private equity investors. The rules changed, and even entrepreneurs with sound business models and management experience . . . were unable to find financing. The lack of access to capital spelled doom to many budding education entrepreneurs. . . . Who said the investment community was fair?" For-profit investors are as fallible as anyone else, but they also have resources, tools, and incentives that make them potentially invaluable partners in reimagining American education.

Most venture investors rely on extensive networks of friends and business contacts to provide investment opportunities. Venture investors consistently report that they care more about the strengths and bona fides of the entrepreneurial team than about the particulars of the business plan. Some readers may be surprised to learn that the first thing prospective investors typically examine when considering a possible investment is not the entrepreneur's idea but who the founders and managers are, their past accomplishments, and their references. Such networks, of course, are somewhat scarce in schooling.

To achieve high levels of returns and offset potential bankruptcies, venture capital firms normally seek to invest in companies that have the potential to deliver substantial returns—young companies that have the potential to become a Yahoo or Google. Such growth potential is most readily apparent where there is significant opportunity for radical gains in productivity through tools, technology, or new process innovations. In evaluating investments, venture firms typically seek an outsized rate of return—in the ballpark of 500 percent over five years. That works out to an annual return of 35 or 40 percent, or triple what professional investors might seek for investments in public companies. The heightened rate of return that venture investors demand reflects the risks they are taking. Because venture firms expect to lose 30 to 50 percent of their investments, the winners have to make up for that.

This helps explain the dearth of for-profit investment in K–12. One prominent venture capital investor who has enjoyed several successes investing in K–12 firms explained to me why she would prefer never to invest in K–12 again:

> Successful venture investors look for opportunities to leverage intellectual capital in situations where an industry is going through a transformative event—that is, an event that wrecks the economics of big industry players. For example, in computers and communications, there were many opportunities for creative destruction. In K–12, the things that make the system more effective are not in [the] interest of the system. There are too many obstacles against transformation. K–12 is not a free market. It is regulated, unionized, bureaucratic, and highly fragmented.

While some readers may be profoundly uncomfortable with increased for-profit investment in schooling, for-profit activity can yield substantial benefits. As discussed in Chapter 2, for-profits have stronger self-interested reasons than nonprofits to grow, seek cost efficiencies, and tackle newly identified areas of need. This same self-interest can lead too readily to shortsighted and self-serving behavior, but it is hard to make the case that we would be better off as a nation if Apple, eBay, and Whole Foods had remained boutiques or regional operations. Given proper attention to quality control and outcome-based accountability, increased for-profit investment has the potential to fuel the same kind of national successes in K–12.

Greenfield ventures increasingly blur the lines between the nonprofit and for-profit structures. As Ted Mitchell of NewSchools Venture Fund suggests, "We could unlock much more private capital in the education sector" if investors could expect that financial returns and tax breaks would "accompany the social return."[24] One such example exists in North Carolina, where proposed legislation would create a new Low-Profit Limited Liability Partnership Company, or L3C, which would be permitted to generate a modest profit while pursuing charitable or educational goals. Such a change would make it easier for foundations to support for-profit organizations whose primary goal is to serve public ends.[25] The key to attracting private capital away from less-critical sectors and into teaching and learning is both to make the environment more hospitable to creative problem solvers and to find ways for public or philanthropic dollars to complement such investment.

It's Not Just Dollars—It's Infrastructure, Too

Dollars alone are not enough. Just as talent does not emerge or mature in a vacuum, new and growing ventures require more than money. They need access to professional networks that can introduce them to clients, provide technical advice on questions like finances and strategy, and offer mentoring and seasoned advice on leadership and management. Foundations and would-be reformers have too often ignored this in K–12 education, investing in promising pilot programs only to be puzzled when the founder proved ill-equipped to expand into promising new locales, procure facilities, hire new school leaders, or secure suppliers. On this count, the experience of the KIPP Academies is instructive. As the KIPP operation grew from a single school to more than 70, philanthropist and business magnate Don Fischer, who was instrumental in funding their growth, provided access to his expertise and network while pushing the founders to build a professional staff to oversee the organization's growth.

Reformers and funders need to provide not just money, but also a trellis that can offer necessary support to new ventures and some protection until they are strong enough to stand on their own. Vanessa Kirsch, founder of the venture philanthropy fund New Profit Inc., has tellingly noted that organizations in which New Profit invests often find the strategic and technical assistance at least as important as the infusion of funds. The New York City Center for Charter School Excellence, the National Alliance for Public Charter Schools, and New Schools for New Orleans, all discussed earlier, are terrific examples of how to marry dollars to mentoring, expertise, networks, and quality control.

Another intriguing example is the Indianapolis-based nonprofit The Mind Trust (TMT), founded in 2006 to promote educational entrepreneurship. TMT's unique Education Entrepreneur Fellowship serves as an incubator for new ventures, offering a $90,000 salary for two years, full benefits, office space, and customized support to a few fellows a year. The 2009 fellowship competition garnered more than 300 proposals, which addressed curricula, professional development, instruction, and school models and were crafted by applicants who had a slew of advanced degrees and stunning resumes and came from inside and outside the K–12 sector. Fellowship winners incubate their ventures in Indianapolis and other cities across the United States.

TMT also operates a venture fund that has successfully attracted some existing entrepreneurial organizations—including Teach For America, The New Teacher Project, and College Summit—to set up shop in Indianapolis. The venture fund provides both dollars and a framework of support, cultivating a strong network of enterprising schooling talent and energy in the city of Indianapolis and paralleling what the technology industry has done in Boston and San Francisco.

Incubating Excellence

David Harris, CEO of The Mind Trust, explains that getting this endeavor up and running was a learning process: "When we launched The Mind Trust, the Indianapolis Public Schools (IPS) superintendent, Dr. Eugene White, was an enthusiastic supporter, serving on our board and expressing an eagerness to partner with the ventures we were bringing to the city.... But the district administration had little experience working with entrepreneurial partners," and early initiatives were bogged down by bureaucracy, foot-dragging, and confusion about how to proceed.

It soon became clear that IPS needed an internal champion of these innovations, someone who could act on Superintendent White's behalf and move the initiatives forward. Harris recalls, "That's where The Mind Trust came in. We recruited and paid for a former superintendent to assume this role. . . . The Mind Trust continues to pay the cost of the special assistant's services. And that made all the difference: With this advisor leading the way, IPS's central office moved into high gear, and all the initiatives launched on time. This approach continues to pay off as we bring additional ventures to town, help our fellows start up their initiatives, and troubleshoot."

New ventures face hurdles, and TMT helps knock them down. Harris explains, "We brought Diploma Plus to town, an organization that runs very successful schools for over-age, undercredited students. One of the reasons Diploma Plus is so successful is that it designs its schools to work for its student population's specific needs. But this means changing schedules, allowing for early release time for working students, and using different kinds of teachers—all of which run up against traditional state and district rules." So TMT worked with the state board of education to craft the necessary waivers.

When it comes to clearing barriers, Harris says, "We know our city so well that we are able to make all kinds of connections and matches that help the ventures thrive. . . . We've made countless introductions that have opened doors for our ventures to find board members and advisors, raise money, and create all kinds of partnerships." For instance, TMT connected Earl Martin Phalen with the superintendent of the Metropolitan School Districts of Decatur Township, which resulted in the district piloting Phalen's Summer Advantage USA program. TMT also connected Phalen to key officials at the Indiana Department of Education, resulting in a million-dollar state investment in the program.

TMT also hustles to enhance the image of its initiatives and fellows. Harris notes, "We've raised the profile of our fellows and venture fund partners by connecting all of them to key media. An *Indianapolis Star* columnist has profiled all four fellows in multiple columns on The Mind Trust's Fellowship. The Mind Trust has also worked with allies in Indianapolis to host multiple receptions and dinners to introduce our fellows to community leaders. As a result of one of these events, Celine Coggins, a fellow [whom we met in Chapter 2], formed a relationship with a key Indianapolis leader who is aggressively raising money for her initiative."

Finally, and obviously, TMT has invested $4 million in its initiatives and has helped them raise hundreds of thousands of dollars from other national and local funders. Ultimately, though, the money is only one piece of the puzzle. As Harris cautions, "The Mind Trust's strong ties to the philanthropic, business, and political communities of Indianapolis allow us to support our partners and fellows in myriad nonfinancial ways, too . . . [and] building this support, mobilizing a whole community of local champions, and connecting them with the entrepreneurs is what will ensure that our short-term investments pay long-term dividends."

Conclusion

The importance of money is self-evident. Less obvious is that it also matters where that money comes from and what kind of scaffolding accompanies it. Ultimately, creating greenfield is not just about the money itself, but also about the networks, expertise, quality control, and availability of support throughout a new venture's life cycle. As noted in Chapter 4, one severe problem for investors is the lack of good data on the cost and performance of various K–12 providers, as this makes it hard to judge the relative quality or promise of potential investments. Effective markets require that dollars follow performance, which in turn requires nuanced, high-quality data. Various advances are helping to meet the need for data and performance metrics.

One such example is the Web-based Portfolio Data Management System, developed by the Acumen Fund. The system helps foundations and grantmakers set benchmarks for measuring social impact and tracking grantees' performances, and allows funders to compare performance of various nonprofits doing similar work. The tool enables foundations to monitor the nonprofits' and their grantees' revenues and outlays; operational metrics, like the number of teachers recruited or assessments conducted; and social metrics, like the organization's impact on student achievement or behavior.

Another complication caused by the predominance of nonprofits in K–12 is the absence of mergers and acquisitions, in which promising new ventures are acquired and then scaled up by providers with established networks. In fields like software or biotech, proud founders are enticed to relinquish their autonomy or control in return for lucrative rewards. This frees successful entrepreneurs to plunge back into new ventures with their newfound resources. In K–12, there is little to encourage entrepreneurs to entrust their handiwork to someone else or to prompt several similar efforts to combine in the name of heightened quality and efficiency. The creator of a charter school or talent provider is routinely still at the helm a decade later—whether or not his or her skills are well-suited to the challenges of sustaining, rather than building, an enterprise.

Because nearly all education spending consists of public expenditures, greenfield depends on whether public dollars allow schools and districts to work with entrepreneurial providers. One program that fosters such cooperation is the federal Teacher Incentive Fund, in which districts pursuing performance-based teacher and principal pay in high-need schools can compete for funds. Those dollars have prompted states and districts to reach out to entrepreneurial organizations like the Teacher Advancement Project, which has developed a promising and professionalized teacher pay and evaluation system.

Reshaping public funding practices is critical to enabling successful, high-quality entrepreneurial organizations to grow. Joe Keeney and Daniel Pianko have suggested that such strategies might entail bonuses for performance, or prizes for breakthrough outcomes.[26] States, for example, could alter formulas to increase funding based on each graduate who passes a state exit exam or goes on to enroll in postsecondary education. This could spur districts to seek entrepreneurial partners with a track record of success on that score, such as College Summit.

Investment in K–12 is limited by regulations, funding systems, technology, and norms. The same forces that stifle entrepreneurs can also discourage funders from choosing to invest in these ventures. In the end, money and the accompanying infrastructure are essential to creating vibrant greenfield. When investors perceive that effective startups have a plausible path to success, and when they see a viable market and supportive statutory and regulatory environments, both big-hearted foundations and gimlet-eyed investors are far more likely to put their dollars to work—and that will determine how well and how widely new ventures can serve students, educators, and schools.

7

GETTING STARTED

WHY GREENFIELD SCHOOLING? Why a whole book about ideas and practices without a single prescription for *classroom* practice? Because our conventional approaches to school reform have not delivered and are not likely to deliver. Greenfield reformers believe that the goal of providing high-quality teaching and learning for every child simply cannot be met within our current arrangements. There is simply no way to get there from here. Instead, we must take a big step back from the smug certainties of best practices and instructional leadership in order to take a giant leap forward; we must back away from our established ways of doing business and allow 21st century solutions to emerge.

Taking a step back requires eschewing the conviction that we simply need to get serious about professional development; embrace "data-driven decision making" and rigorous standards; or settle on the right curricula, pedagogies, and assessments. The problem is not that any of these claims are incorrect. They all make good sense on their own terms. The problem is that we keep trying to graft these onto state and district systems that are predisposed to reject the transplant.

Back in Chapter 2, I quoted Friedrich von Hayek's observation that one can approach public policy as either a gardener or engineer. Given the passion and sense of urgency that are so prevalent in schooling, there is an instinctual tendency for policymakers, researchers, and educators to operate as engineers, presuming that we can "fix" the problems by settling upon and mandating the right set of solutions. Unfortunately, such impatience leads us to enthusiastically erect one grand new solution after another rather than preparing the fields that can support viable, sustainable solutions. The great thing about engineering is that we can dust off our hands and announce, "We're done, problem solved!"— even if our brilliant design is soon sinking into the mire. Gardening requires more patience and discipline; it requires that each year we roll up our sleeves and once more clear away the weeds and rubble; seed and plant; and battle the pests. But if one believes, as I do, that our system of schooling is fundamentally unable to support and leverage new tools, technology, or approaches in a useful way, and that even "successful" system reforms yield disheartening results, it is gardening that promises a more serious and sustainable course.

The biggest challenge we face is not a lack of potential practices or good ideas, but systemic rigidity that makes it difficult to execute even smart solutions with discipline and focus. This is not unique to schooling or school systems. In the course of time, even today's most entrepreneurial new ventures will eventually grow ossified—requiring a new wave of creative, nimble successors. The greenfield solution is not to celebrate a handful of name brands or to launch a few new ventures and declare, "Mission accomplished." Rather, it is to create a world of teaching and learning marked by talented people pursuing new and effective ways to serve students, teachers, and schools.

Matt Candler makes this point in typically colorful language. "Most districts are barely, barely creeping [forward], and they're not even close to closing [the achievement] gap," he argues. "My perspective, as a teacher, is that that sucks. I've been in the charter movement for 10 years—this sucks less, but this still sucks. We can't build a [charter school] movement by bragging about marginal improvements on the absurdly low performance of others, yet we act that way at times, bragging about being slightly better than the system that's failed kids for decades. This isn't about being less horrible than someone else, it is about the urgent need to fix a busted system that's failing kids every day."[1] In his book *Whatever It Takes*, which profiles Geoffrey Canada's struggle to create the acclaimed Harlem Children's Zone, journalist Paul Tough vividly captures Canada's motivation. "We're not interested in saving a hundred kids," Canada explains. "Even three hundred kids. Even a thousand kids to me is not going to do it. We want to be able to talk about how you save kids by the tens of thousands, because that's how we're losing them. We're losing kids by the tens of thousands."[2]

Millions and Millions Served

As we noted in Chapter 1, entrepreneurship is both more humble and more ambitious than best practice reform. Even when pointing to the approach of this or that venture in the preceding pages, the aim has not been to hold up one "best practice" or another but only to highlight how agile organizations can find better ways to solve stubborn problems. Humility dictates that entrepreneurs embrace outcomes and judge their success on the extent to which they *promote new efficiencies, address unmet needs, or perform consistently at high levels*. This is the first bar that new ventures must clear.

It is not enough, however, for an entrepreneurial venture to simply be good. The second bar is the entrepreneurial imperative *to replicate and to grow*. This is where the ambition enters in. Even though greenfielders know how challenging it is to successfully launch even a single school or to provide a boutique service, they measure themselves against a much more demanding standard: not merely whether their innovation might plausibly be scaled but whether they can use it to deliver transformative benefits to a broad swath of children, families, and educators.

The third bar is for significant entrepreneurial ventures to be *cost-effective*. Entrepreneurs who succeed by adopting a "more, better" strategy can make a valuable contribution, but their impact is inevitably limited. In the same way, schools that rely on scarce talent or extraordinary support hit ceilings when those resources are exhausted. The most compelling entrepreneurial ventures are those that find ways to deliver average or above-average results for less money and with less manpower. *In short, all entrepreneurial ventures are not created equal*. The most significant will be those that are cost-effective and can be replicated at scale. These solutions have the power to transform schooling.

In practice, reformers and philanthropists tend to skip past these three standards. They disproportionately favor boutique ventures, even when it's likely these will be difficult to scale. Indeed, the very traits that fuel early success and make new boutique models attractive and initially promising—a reliance on a "more, better" approach, philanthropic support, and extraordinarily talented and passionate employees—often hinder prospects for growth.

In considering the potential scalability and effect of a given venture, there are at least three key factors to weigh. First, how fierce are the political and institutional barriers that confront this innovation? What are the formal and informal barriers that must be addressed? Ventures that can fly under the radar have an easier path to startup and scalability than those that will meet opposition at every turn, and those that face fewer legal or regulatory hurdles will find it easier to grow.

Second, are there metrics that can gauge the appropriate outcomes? Those innovations that fit most cleanly into the metrics at hand (e.g., reading and math scores in grades 3–8) have enjoyed an enormous leg up in recent years. But if we want to encourage ventures focused on other students, subjects, or needs, additional metrics are essential. If those metrics can be devised and standardized, scalability becomes much more manageable.

Finally, how replicable is the core innovation? Computer simulations, Web-based tutorials, or tightly scripted programs may be much easier to replicate than a school, service, or product that depends heavily on talent. Instructional or school models, on the other hand, have many more variables and are much more dependent on the quality of the instructors and classroom culture—which means that consistent quality requires finding thousands of teachers as committed and skilled as the first handful.

All of this said, Steven Wilson, entrepreneur and author of *Learning on the Job*, reminds us that it's essential to avoid drawing simplistic conclusions as to which ventures are most promising, significant, or readily replicated. For instance, he has made the case that school builders like KIPP are pioneering radical advances in management practice and staffing even when they suggest they are simply employing a "more, better" strategy, and that these advances are educationally more significant than many instances of current technology utilization. He suggests that school builders like KIPP or Achievement First are having a bigger demonstrated impact on student learning than most tool builders or human capital ventures. It is useful to recognize that there is no pat formula by which to gauge the promise of various ventures; making those judgments will and should inevitably be imperfect, context-dependent efforts to apply the relevant standards.

Thinking Beyond the "Whole School"

In Chapter 2, we discussed the limits implicit in the "whole school" mind-set. If the success of new school models is due largely to culture, strong leadership, or a cadre of committed teachers, it is unclear how readily that success can be emulated or replicated. Leaders of effective schools are so good because they are passionate about their interaction with students and faculty; they enjoy the personalized nature of their work. But they may simply be hesitant to leave the site to start over on a whole new replication. And if the recipe for scale is that we need to find and prepare more such leaders, the question that arises is how easy and how feasible that course might be.

Often, what sets a given school apart is not actually the whole school but a particular program or instructional model within it. For instance, an elementary school may be great because of its approach to language immersion. Rather than trying to "replicate" such a school, it might be worth trying to distill that program and build an organization that can execute it widely and with fidelity. Doing so has the effect of narrowing the innovation in question, making it easier to refine and deliver and less dependent on the vagaries of talent.

Moving away from a single-minded focus on "whole school" reform has another benefit. It permits reformers to contemplate strategies that can minimize the disruptive effect of entrepreneurial displacement on students and families. The failure of a tool builder or a recruiter does not pose the same concerns as closing a school does. Meanwhile, tapping service or talent providers to augment or even replace key system functions—such as data management or human resources—could allow districts to gradually remake themselves without inconveniencing families or children.

Allowing ourselves to think beyond the "whole school" also permits us to focus on the kinds of critical supports and structures needed to support new providers—whether they are providing schools, tools, or talent. Because today's systems are balky and outdated, district human resources, information technology, data management, and professional development too rarely support excellence. As soon as greenfield ventures reach a degree of scale, they rapidly learn that it is necessary to recreate these supports. So we see even school builders like Aspire and Achievement First scrambling to build better data systems, expand their recruiting and human resources operations, and provide centralized support.

No one should imagine that greenfield ventures alleviate the need for these services. In fact, many talent providers, tool builders, and service providers are primarily in the business of delivering these very services more effectively. The trick, in the words of KIPP CEO Mike Feinberg, is to do this without replicating "the beast" of central administration.[3] This may entail high-quality new providers like The New Teacher Project providing support across a wealth of locales or districts finding ways to revitalize their operations so that they can support both traditional and new schools.

For Would-Be Entrepreneurs

Across the land, there are practitioners and reformers seeking to launch new schools, provide new curricula, and offer improved training and professional development, in addition to a host of other services we have yet to imagine. We should not for one moment assume that any of these efforts will necessarily make sense or deliver the goods, but we should entertain the possibility and ensure that smart, talented problem solvers have the opportunity to succeed.

If you think you want to be an entrepreneur, the first rule of thumb is to check your assumptions. We have heard in these pages from more than a few successful entrepreneurs as well as many involved in the leading entrepreneurial ventures in education today. Consider the stress, demands, and uncertainty, and whether you really have the skills and temperament for the work. If you are still eager to move forward, the first step is to learn more. The following sidebar offers a few suggestions on where to start.

Getting Started as an Entrepreneur: Practical Advice from the Experts

Creating a business plan. Few aspects of venture creation attract as much attention as the business plan. At a basic level, the business plan is a formal statement of objectives, the reasons why they are achievable, and the path for reaching those goals. While it is helpful to include figures about the scale of the enterprise—such as estimated revenues, costs, and profits—it is most important to clearly articulate a vision for how and why it can be successful. In an influential *Harvard Business Review* article, Harvard Business School professor William Sahlman advises that successful business plans should address four key factors: (1) *the people*, discussing the men and women involved and why they are uniquely suited to start this venture; (2) *the opportunity*, explaining how fast the venture can grow and what main obstacles stand in its way; (3) *the context*, explaining what factors are out of an entrepreneur's hands and how those challenges might be confronted; and (4) *risk and reward*, making the case that the likely benefits outweigh the costs and risks.[4]

Building a team. More important than any other element of a venture are the people involved in it. Recruiting talent, building a culture of excellence, and retaining effective employees are vital to navigating the challenges of a startup. For an entrepreneur, the key is to promote a structure that not only brings in fresh talent but also creates a culture that enables, assists, and encourages employees to excel. In his best-selling book *Good to Great*, nationally recognized consultant Jim Collins suggested that almost every successful enterprise had "level 5 leadership" during its pivotal transition from a good company to a great one. These are entrepreneurs who, through a unique combination of personal humility and professional determination, fostered an atmosphere of achievement in their organizations—by benchmarking and measuring success, hiring and nurturing talent ("getting the right people on the bus"), requiring concentration and discipline (the "hedgehog concept"), and getting the "flywheel" spinning in the right direction—thereby attracting better teams and enhancing performance.[5]

Securing funding. Plenty of entrepreneurs start with a great business plan and talented people and still have difficulty getting off the ground. Usually, the reason is a misunderstanding about how funding works or how it can be secured. Kim Smith, former CEO of the NewSchools Venture Fund, reminds us that new enterprises need three types of money: (1) *startup capital* to hire a team, develop products and services, rent an office, buy supplies, and prepare to launch the business; (2) *growth capital* to support the organization once it is up and running; and (3) *sustaining capital* to finance substantial expansion of the organization. Startup cash is typically obtained through personal financing, loans and other debt instruments, philanthropic support, or venture capital. Public funding for such ventures is rarely available. Which of these resources entrepreneurs should choose depends on the organization's business model, its theory of how it will enact change, the status of the capital markets, and the founder's personal preferences and goals.[6]

Pursuing effective marketing strategies. Every venture realizes that in order to survive, it must acquire and keep customers. In "Building Loyalty in Business Markets," a *Harvard Business Review* article that every aspiring entrepreneur should read, Harvard Business School professor Das Narayandas argues that enterprises must begin their marketing and selling by asking the basic vision question: *What businesses are we in?* From there, entrepreneurs can more readily deploy branding techniques, develop communication tactics, and pinpoint sales tools. The challenge, in every instance, is for the enterprise to make the case for why its product is more desirable than others. This usually takes the form of product differentiation, lower prices, or a better business-client relationship. Ultimately, Narayandas says, the aim for any venture should be to build a customer base characterized by a willingness to do six things: (1) *grow the relationship* (buy more products); (2) *provide word-of-mouth endorsements* (talk about the venture positively); (3) *resist competitors' blandishments* (refuse to switch brands); (4) *pay premiums* (pay higher prices); (5) *collaborate* (offer feedback to improve products and services); and (6) *invest* (provide funds to grow the company).

Organizations that create a business plan, build an effective team, secure funding, and pursue effective marketing strategies will be well positioned to add value, meet client needs, and look forward to new challenges and opportunities.[7]

Now, I am an academic and not an entrepreneur, but when aspiring entrepreneurs ask me for advice, I do have a few bits I sometimes share. First, remember that success means sustaining your effort and being able to expand it to eventually serve more children, educators, schools, or systems. This will require both resources and clients. Fortunately, there is a huge appetite among educators and funders for programs that offer some demonstrable evidence of success, so evidence of effectiveness can open doors and help secure resources.

The second, related point is that viability and growth require showing success, but it is hard to make that case without resources and pilot sites. This can present a frustrating paradox for entrepreneurs. To solve this chicken-and-egg dilemma, entrepreneurs need to be scrappy about locating initial resources, finding sites to test their idea, and collecting data to demonstrate that their venture has merit.

One venture that successfully resisted the temptation to settle for a succession of small-scale pilots and benefited enormously was the Grow Network, a startup that interprets high-stakes test data for parents, teachers, and principals and is now a division of McGraw-Hill. Grow Network founder David Coleman refused to offer pilots and insisted on citywide contracts. Although this represented an enormous risk, it meant that the contracts Grow did win would enable the company to focus on being successful at scale. As Coleman puts it, "Building for scale transformed our product development and professional development from the beginning. We knew that since we were working with 4,000 teachers, we couldn't make a thick, difficult product that required in-depth, one-on-one training. This approach is very different from building something that will work in one school and hoping it will go to scale." He points out that an overreliance on promising pilot models creates the risk that we will focus on solutions that only work at the school level and are not readily scalable.[8]

Third, from the outset, entrepreneurs need to be aggressive and strategic about collecting data and documenting their impact. Fortunately, there is a whole population constantly seeking significant new programs and ventures to evaluate and study: graduate students and university professors. New opportunities are particularly appealing to young academics seeking to stake out fresh turf. In return for exclusive access, entrepreneurs can get both the independent data and empirical analysis they need. This requires settling on metrics that are credible and that make sense, collecting the data, and ensuring that the data are analyzed. Evidence of effectiveness can open doors and help secure resources.

Fourth, when the results are strong, it is vital for entrepreneurs to disseminate the evaluations of their efforts. Potential clients must be made aware of them. This kind of "marketing" is second nature for big corporations and snake oil artists but can seem a distraction to the most passionate and focused entrepreneurs. It can be well worth the time and energy to try to ensure that evaluations and studies are disseminated through scholarly journals, widely read education publications like *Educational Leadership* and *Education Week*, Web sites and blogs, and presentations to groups like the National School Boards Association and the Council of Great City Schools.

Fifth, entrepreneurs must think strategically about targets of opportunity. For instance, charter schools can be frustrating for service or talent providers to work with because most are isolated units that are unable to purchase a service at scale. Ideally, any entrepreneur would rather work with systems large enough that supplying them is economically viable. This was the principle that David Coleman held to so fiercely when launching the Grow Network. The need to win access to some sites may argue for compromise. Charter schools, in particular, can be an attractive resource because they have fewer chokepoints to frustrate new providers and are less susceptible to turnover in the superintendent's office. There is no universal rule here. Each entrepreneur must gauge his or her own circumstances.

Finally, remember the advantage of ventures that can be scaled cost-effectively. Entrepreneurial endeavors that are highly dependent on talent, passion, and committed staff tend to be the most successful but also the least equipped to expand rapidly or operate on a grand scale. Models reliant on limited resources, like phenomenal talent or philanthropic support, will always be more difficult to expand than models that leverage more plentiful resources. New ventures should always have one eye on the question of how their work might "scale"—or should seek R&D partners who will do this for them.

For Teachers

For teachers frustrated by the passion for silver bullets, undisciplined leadership, simple-minded approaches to testing, or the persistent failure of new instructional and curricular approaches, greenfield thinking offers a promising way forward. Because greenfield reform is so focused on systems, institutions, and changes outside the classroom door, however, even sympathetic teachers can wonder, "What does all of this have to do with me? If I'm not about to become an entrepreneur tomorrow, what can I do?" The short answer is "a lot."

The voices of teachers, as members of school systems and the profession, are critical to promoting greenfield. Given union resistance to so many greenfield proposals, the understandable skepticism of veterans who have seen so many reforms come and go without making a dent, and general suspicion toward outsiders and nontraditional educators, teachers have the potential to be enormously influential advocates for change. The power of educators standing up and making the case for greenfield is not to be underestimated, nor is the ability of practitioners to lend invaluable expertise and experience to crafting these efforts. There is substantial interest in learning from and empowering entrepreneurially minded educators—whether it entails DCPS chancellor Michelle Rhee hiring former national teacher of the year Jason Kamras to design the district's teacher evaluation plan, former Denver Public Schools superintendent (now U.S. Senator) Michael Bennet hiring Denver Education Association official Brad Jupp to work on teacher quality, or former Cambridge, Milwaukee, and Detroit schools administrator Deborah McGriff being snatched up to be a vice president at Edison Schools and then a partner at the NewSchools Venture Fund.

Perhaps it is less important whether one buys into the entire greenfield argument than that one uses a greenfield lens to consider the panoply of familiar reforms. One need not entirely embrace the critique of best practice reform, but certainly there are benefits to be gained from subjecting our present world of schooling—its various institutions, rules, and routines—to healthy scrutiny. If our biggest challenge is not *this* pedagogy or *that* curriculum but the very system *itself*, then teachers must make themselves heard.

For those with whom the greenfield case resonates, there are three things to keep in mind. First, there is the potential for new school models and instructional delivery (whether online tutoring or Citizen Schools–style adjuncting) to let teachers develop and find new roles that better suit their skills, circumstances, and interests. One such example is offered by the EdVisions co-op model now employed by several dozen schools in Minnesota, Wisconsin, and California, in which teacher-partners manage the school without hierarchical leadership. Alternatively, finding new roles for educators might also allow a teacher to opt to be a stay-at-home parent but still work 20 to 30 hours per week for an online tutoring firm. Whatever the specifics, teachers can push to see that they have expanding professional opportunities and that they are designed with an eye toward smart problem solving and excellence.

Second, there is a need to discard the factory model in favor of a more professional standard. Excessive standardization of pay scales, duties, and training denies educators the opportunities to be recognized for their efforts and creates a profession more attuned to the rhythms of a 20th century automobile plant than a magnet for educated talent. The resulting opportunities for educators are enormous—as illustrated by the Equity Project Charter School, a New York City charter that opened in 2009 and pays faculty an annual salary of $125,000. The school managed that feat with no additional resources aside from fresh thinking and a decision to boost class sizes to about 30. The model takes professionalism seriously, with an extended professional work day that includes daily peer observations, an annual six-week Summer Development Institute, and a sabbatical every five or six years to foster professional growth.[9] Teachers can support the creation of more such models—and teacher voices advocating them will go a long way toward countering the skepticism or hostility of entrenched opponents.

Finally, there is a need to push school, district, and political leaders to lower barriers and make it possible for educators and problem solvers to rethink the work of teaching and learning. These educational leaders and officials are used to thinking of teachers as change-averse. They routinely hear from teacher associations, which disproportionately represent the interests of teachers skeptical of dramatic change. Those teachers comfortable with greenfield-style reform need to communicate their preferences forcefully and let the public know that some educators welcome this kind of rethinking.

For District Leaders

Education is different from a field like software design in that there is not much natural greenfield; the land has been pretty thoroughly paved over, meaning that greenfield has to be recreated by superintendents and other public officials. That is why greenfield districts such as New York City, New Orleans, Indianapolis, and Washington, DC, are so important today. These experiences show how far a single superintendent and supportive community can go toward creating an entrepreneurial hotbed. Since there is probably need for only a limited number of entrepreneurial hotbeds in education, there is an enormous opportunity for the communities that move first and most aggressively.

District leaders can gain significant competitive advantages by making their systems more talent-friendly. This requires fighting to lower state licensure barriers and district hiring processes that discourage candidates or recruit through too narrow a screen. Once hired, teachers and education leaders need the freedom and flexibility to identify challenges, diagnose situations, and take action. Of course, granting this kind of freedom requires rolling back procedural rules and replacing them with a system of accountability premised on performance and competition. Teachers need opportunities to grow professionally, advance in their careers, and know that their energy and entrepreneurial spirit will be recognized.

Joe Williams, president of Democrats for Education Reform, has explained that entrepreneurial district leaders understand "that radically altering the path of large school systems requires changes to nearly every piece of the system's puzzle. Functions like hiring and human resources are recognized as being crucial ingredients in terms of improving what happens in classrooms." He notes, for instance, that New York City's labor relations team has become a crucial part of the district's reform effort and "in addition to creating new lessons for principals about how to better handle teacher evaluations to make them more grievance-proof, the legal team has helped shape policy to usher in improvements." Williams also points out that even though New York City had run summer school programs for years, when Chancellor Joel Klein created the Summer Success Academy, he labeled it a "new" program so his team could sidestep the standard practice of making summer school assignments based on seniority.[10]

District leaders looking to create greenfield can start by embracing information and technological advancements that lower geographical barriers to the provision of instruction, support services, and professional development. Making their systems more attractive and open to these entrepreneurial reforms starts with three steps. First, they should aggressively tackle the kinds of formal and informal barriers discussed in Chapter 3. Leaders must champion creative problem solving while making it clear to the board, civic leadership, and school leaders that neither routines nor inherited policies should be an excuse for poor performance or inefficiency. This involves tapping external expertise to ensure that the procurement process is well managed, making decisions in a transparent and quality-conscious manner, and basing decisions on reliable assessments of cost-effectiveness. Leaders need to look to new vendors and technologies not merely in terms of instructional outcomes, but also with an eye toward cost efficiencies and determining whether new tools make it possible to discard outdated practices or tackle challenges in smarter ways.

Boards and district leaders must honor hard-charging leaders and stand firmly behind them in the face of inevitable reversals. Principals must be pushed to make smart, quality conscious personnel decisions—and to act on them, whether that entails reassignment or termination—even when those decisions spur conflict and even though some won't pan out.

Second, greenfield leaders need to take a page from New York City Department of Education chancellor Joel Klein's book and push to turn their system into a "Silicon Valley" of school reform.[11] They can nurture networks and scaffolding by championing city-based efforts like New Schools for New Orleans or The Mind Trust in Indianapolis. They can aid in the search for talent and dollars by working to attract The New Teacher Project or Education Pioneers and by reaching out to venture philanthropists like the NewSchools Venture Fund. They should also work with funders and state officials to make facilities available to new providers and to erect the kinds of supports and resources that can make such efforts successful.

Finally, greenfield leaders should make it a priority to develop balanced scorecards that measure the efficiency and cost-effectiveness of key district services and functions. They can look to pioneering work done on this count by the Council of Great City Schools or consulting firms like McKinsey & Company and Bain & Company. When it comes to data and quality assurance, it is not enough to claim to be "data-driven." Districts should invest in information technology that provides data on student and teacher performance, expenditures, and personnel. The goal cannot be simply tracking whether student achievement is rising but knowing whether individual providers, schools, and educators are doing their jobs well and whether they are doing so cost-effectively.

One Vision of School Systems Transformed

Approaching the challenge in this way creates vast opportunities for fresh thinking. In *Crash Course: A Radical Plan for Improving Public Education*, Edison Schools (now EdisonLearning) founder Chris Whittle sketches a vision of what schooling might look like in 2030. He frames the exercise with this question: "So if we suspend our disbelief, if we apply the dynamics and rates of change commonplace in other arenas, if we think, as other industries do, that transformation is a prerequisite for survival, what could our school systems (and the companies that will serve them) look like in 2030?" He offers some provocative thoughts.

New York City, 2030. Whittle imagines extensive partnerships with school management companies that reassign responsibilities among districts and providers. For management companies, he writes, "Each company had complete management responsibility for its schools, including curriculum, instruction, finances, cleaning, food, and enrollment. . . . Each company had substantial incentives and penalties tied to student achievement. Though the contracts were twenty years in length, they could be terminated if a company failed over any three-year period to reach achievement targets."

For districts, he suggests, "The school district maintained all the key overarching system-management responsibilities," including hiring the providers, assessments, funding, facilities, parent involvement, and teacher collective bargaining agreements. "The district left day-to-day operation of the schools to the companies."

Middleburg, Tennessee, 2030. Whittle posits that the model in New York City did not translate well to rural America as "smaller districts . . . found it difficult or unworkable to divide them among different providers. And the companies themselves found it economically and operationally challenging to manage a single school or even several remote sites." But Middleburg's superintendent instead imported the providers' school design.

Rather than privatization, Whittle imagines a partnership model with a single provider. "Middleburg School District would be the boss," "Middleburg would continue to 'own' its school facilities and provide core services such as maintenance, transportation, and food service," and "Middleburg would continue as the fiduciary."

He sees providers delivering "twelve key services to the district, ones where scale was a key determinant of excellence." Providers would assist with recruiting teachers and professional development and organizing and managing the school's central office. Whittle explains, "In some respects, the relationship between [a provider] and its affiliate districts is similar to that of major television networks, in which the local stations are owned and operated by local entrepreneurs but have relationships with major national networks for their national programming and news."[12]

For Advocates and Policymakers

The temptation for reformers and public officials is to champion "surefire" solutions to our educational challenges. But if we take a step back, we realize that we do not ask gubernatorial candidates how they will ensure an automobile factory or insurance firm becomes more productive; instead, we ask candidates what broader actions they will take to help firms prosper, respect the public's needs, and create jobs. When it comes to schools, however, we too often expect public officials to become engineers and to sketch out solutions in detail.

We would all do well to take Friedrich von Hayek's advice and ask leaders to think more like gardeners and less like engineers. What can they do to reduce obstacles; foster smart private and public quality control; and promote talent, capital, and networks? What laws, outdated and ill-suited for the 21st century, might they strip from the books? What rules governing textbook procurement or teacher credentials might they rethink?

Too many greenfield sympathizers underestimate the need to build the political power that will change the rules, regulations, and habits that get in their way. Others are overly optimistic that the regulatory environment will somehow reform itself after seeing good results from early supply-side work. The premise is that policymakers will lower formal barriers once successes assuage public opinion and skittish officials. Walton Family Foundation official Ed Kirby has dismissively labeled such thinking as "reform by enlightenment"—the hope that if entrepreneurs build a better mousetrap, opposition will melt away, and policymakers will embrace it. In theory, the strategy sounds great. In reality, it consistently disappoints.[13] Because today's limited pool of entrepreneurs has generally set up shop in a handful of reasonably hospitable markets, observers can be forgiven for wondering whether their efforts are inherently small scale, and even ad hoc. Because entrepreneurs have incentives to step and speak gingerly, their achievements are sometimes used to excuse existing arrangements. This is particularly true in districts where entrepreneurs operate outstanding schools inside or in partnership with districts. In these cases, the occasional success is not reason to say, "See, these obstacles aren't so onerous after all." The irony is that the extraordinary efforts of those few entrepreneurs able to negotiate a burdensome status quo can be used to defend it—and the nature of the entrepreneurs' position is that they reap autonomy, resources, recruits, and recognition by staying mum and quietly standing as a Potemkin village.

There is an intense need for third parties that can make the entrepreneurs' case in ways those in the field cannot. It is essential that advocates and policymakers raise the impolite truths that entrepreneurs find difficult to say and explain what it will take to drive transformative change. This is the case even when the entrepreneurs themselves would prefer to tiptoe around the hard truths. Statewide advocacy groups, like ConnCAN (Connecticut Coalition for Achievement Now) in Connecticut and EdVoice in California, and national groups, like the National Alliance for Public Charter Schools, provide illustrative models. These organizations avoid advocating for new "musts"—such as insisting that teachers have this credential or that districts must maintain that class size. They instead focus on removing barriers and ensuring that new problem solvers have the opportunity to succeed.

Hard-nosed advocacy can seem tedious to those who just want to help kids or who have a distaste for conflict. A natural tendency is to latch onto solutions that promise to sidestep this hard work. Twenty years ago, the hot, new one-step solution was school vouchers. Today, it can too often be technology, which has potential to transform schooling but will not do so on its own.

For example, in 2008, Harvard Business School professor Clayton Christensen published *Disrupting Class*, a provocative and influential volume that applied many of the insights from his previous work on disruptive innovation to schooling. Christensen argued that Web-based learning is so accessible, convenient, and cost-effective that it will inevitably start displacing traditional K–12 course instruction. However, those who have enthusiastically embraced the volume have frequently failed to consider how barriers and the structure of schooling may stifle disruptive K–12 innovation or how organizational incentives matter for the ways in which technology is utilized.[14] In his earlier research, Christensen focused on for-profit firms in a marketplace where the old giants wanted to maximize returns and emerging ventures were hungry for market share. The complementary incentives yielded an elegant waltz toward Schumpeterian innovation.[15]

There is much cause to be skeptical that those dynamics will play out similarly in the barrier-strewn, politicized, and rule-constricted world of schooling. There is reason to ask if states and school districts, with access to the public purse and hemmed in by constituent demands, will respond to new providers in the same fashion as dominant for-profit corporations eager to maintain their profitability.

It can be tempting for would-be reformers to latch onto technology, school choice, or some other deus ex machina that will naturally and inevitably circumvent the obstacles that have frustrated entrepreneurs for so long. That mistake is similar to the one that the scholars John Chubb and Terry Moe made in the profoundly influential *Politics, Markets, and America's Schools*, when they famously, but incorrectly, opined two decades ago: "Without being too literal about it, we think reformers would do well to entertain the notion that choice is a panacea. . . . It has the capacity all by itself to bring about the kind of transformation that, for years, reformers have been seeking to engineer in myriad other ways."[16] The unfulfilled promise of such claims illustrates why it is important for policymakers and advocates not to imagine that silver bullets (whether technology, professional development models, school choice schemes, or anything else) will somehow suffice, but to focus on removing obstacles, ensuring smart quality control, and cultivating key resources—in other words, the work of creating and preparing greenfield.

The paucity and newness of educational entrepreneurship limit its role in altering policy. In the meantime, other voices need to be heard on behalf of wholesale reform strategies. It is wrong to expect successful entrepreneurs to lead that charge, but advocates and policymakers can serve as field marshals for large-scale policy change. Too often, greenfield sympathizers can get caught up in their own pet agendas, whether "teacher quality," "accountability," "school choice," or what have you, and be tone-deaf to the array of real challenges entrepreneurs face.

For Philanthropists

Philanthropists give to K–12 education with the best of intentions: to be good citizens and give our children a more promising future. For many givers, the last thing they want to do is provoke controversy. The frequent result is that most have deferred over time to status quo experts full of good intentions and promise—while shying away from edgy measures that have real potential to upend the system. It is easy for philanthropies to soft-pedal their efforts to promote significant change and to embrace the opportunity to give dollars for professional development to an acclaimed school. This has resulted in what Robin Pasquarella, former president and CEO of the Seattle Alliance for Education, labeled "band-aid giving." Referring to efforts to patch a broken system or make feel-good contributions that may have little impact, Pasquarella observed, "They're random acts of kindness. There's nothing wrong with that. . . . It just doesn't change anything."[17] In fact, band-aid giving can actually be a case where funders or the business community are buying good will with districts and teachers unions, serving to condone and perpetuate a broken system.

A more useful tack is to invest aggressively in research that determines not just which new ventures are effective but *why* they are effective. There is an opportunity for researchers to do a better job of learning from existing ventures. While there is a lot going on to attract entrepreneurial talent and tackle the attendant challenges, these endeavors are often undocumented and under-publicized. Moreover, most research focuses on evaluating charter schools or the effect of TFA corps members, rather than on understanding the obstacles that entrepreneurs face, the measures that help them succeed, or how philanthropists, reformers, and policymakers have helped produce a high-quality supply of education providers. Funding research that peers into that black box, urging grantees to engage in such efforts, and pushing grantees to explore how they might alter their design to be more efficient or take fuller advantage of talent or technology are all things that donors are especially well equipped to do.

Finally, consider how some modest investments in building infrastructure can yield vast new swaths of greenfield. Dr. Muhammad Yunus and his brain-child, the Grameen Bank, were awarded the Nobel Peace Prize in late 2006 for their pioneering work in micro-finance. The Grameen Bank (literally "Bank of the Villages"), launched in 1976 in Bangladesh, was designed to offer banking services and credit to the rural poor. The inability to tap small amounts of capital had traditionally made it difficult for the rural poor to purchase needed equipment or start businesses. The Grameen Bank offered tiny loans, while creating networks of neighbors who could provide needed capital and social support. In 1983, government legislation transformed the Grameen Bank into an independent bank. Since then, the Grameen Bank and its many imitators have sparked a powerful wave of activity in Southeast Asia and elsewhere, even absent dramatic efforts to overhaul an otherwise inhospitable political economy.

For Community and Business Leaders

Other things being equal, community leaders prefer to embrace successful school models and collaborate tranquilly with districts. Rather than focus so relentlessly on backing the status quo, civic and business leaders would do well to adopt as a mission statement the analysis of high schools that Microsoft cofounder Bill Gates offered to the National Governors Association a few years ago. "America's high schools are obsolete," Gates said. "By 'obsolete,' I don't just mean . . . broken, flawed, and underfunded—though a case could be made for every one of those points. By 'obsolete,' I mean that our high schools—even when they're working exactly as designed—cannot teach our kids what they need to know today. . . . This isn't an accident or a flaw in the system; it is the system."[18] Addressing that challenge requires more than donations and quiet support; it requires unflinching and uncompromising community leadership.

What, specifically, can these groups do to help create greenfield and promote breakthrough improvement? First, any vibrant sector requires strong new ventures to have access to venture capital, be able to secure expertise and talent, and have the opportunity to grow. It is not just the lack of resources that deters potential entrepreneurs, but also the lack of networks, mentoring, and a straightforward way to locate investors. One attractive model is the decade-old, San Francisco–based NewSchools Venture Fund, cofounded by venture capitalist John Doerr, which offers funding to new providers while tapping its own network to give strategic planning, financial modeling, and fundraising advice.

Second, creating greenfield will require painful measures to unravel familiar routines and laws. Many changes cannot be enacted simply through collaboration or consensus, and many will require bruising fights and may spark bad feelings. Community and business leaders can lead these fights and provide reform leaders with the political cover they need. Business and civic leaders are key players in local bond drives and other efforts to provide more dollars for schooling, but too often they have given money, muscle, and support without demanding substantial reform in exchange. It is time to strike a savvier bargain. The price of support should be serious movement on fronts such as removing barriers, promoting transparency, pursuing smart quality control, and seeking out cost-effective providers.

Business leaders also have deep expertise in areas like performance evaluation, human resources, information technology, and data systems. Tom Donohue of the U.S. Chamber of Commerce noted that in a 2007 study, "Not a single state could provide systematic data on teacher performance or return on investment. No responsible publicly or privately held firm could operate successfully with such a lack of data. While education policymakers have invested great energy in gathering student achievement data, they have paid inadequate attention to developing the kind of information essential to driving organizational improvement."[19] These are places where business has decades of hard-won experience, and companies can pass on lessons to schools in areas like accountability, compensation, and management that can allow them to serve as the voice of reason when would-be reformers champion ill-conceived notions.

Rejecting a New "One Best System"

Since the 1974 publication of education historian David Tyack's seminal *The One Best System*, many reforms have proceeded from the premise that the factory-inspired school systems we have inherited need to be redesigned.[20] Much of this energy has been fueled by efforts to uncover or design new "best practices" that will yield a new "best" system.

The greenfield premise rejects that aim. The object is not to erect a new One Best System but to erect a system that attracts and supports dynamic problem solvers. The aim is a flexible environment that welcomes talent, focuses on results, rewards success, removes failures, and does not stifle the emergence of new and better solutions. Abandoning the quest for a One Best System requires recognizing the critical difference between embracing entrepreneurship and seeking to institutionalize the practices of admired providers like Uncommon Schools and Aspire Public Schools. Because today's winners represent terrific versions of the standard schoolhouse, seeking to make today's favorites into the new normal will impede providers and hinder the next generation of problem solvers.

Rather than focus on identifying new "best" models, greenfield reform promotes measures that identify and support a variety of effective models while holding the door open for new, superior solutions. Five principles should guide such an endeavor.

First, the system must be dynamic, agile, and responsive to the challenges presented by a changing world. This requires the dissolution of barnacled monopolies and a movement toward systems that are flexible and that do not erect exhausting barriers to new providers. The challenge is to design a system that, 25 years from now, will allow entrepreneurs of that era to focus on solving problems rather than struggling to dismantle the roadblocks that we have unwittingly strewn in their path. Some well-intended measures, such as class size reduction or NCLB's highly qualified teacher provision, have mandated constrictive guidelines that promise to stifle a new generation of problem solvers just as thoroughly as collective bargaining provisions and teacher licensure have hampered today's.

Second, vibrant greenfield is transparent and marked by readily available data on performance, productivity, and finances that hold providers accountable and compel them to compete on cost and quality. Student performance data should not only be readily accessible, but must be usable by policymakers, educators, entrepreneurs, and parents as they seek to make decisions. Beyond that, entrepreneurs and those they serve should be tailoring metrics to measure the services provided and gauge cost-effective performance. This requires moving from a system designed around inputs to one designed around outcomes. Valid, reliable, and sufficiently comprehensive competency-based achievement measures—even when taught online, in unconventional schools, or in ways yet unseen—are a critical part of this, but (as we discussed in Chapter 4) so are good measures of the varied services that districts and providers deliver.

Third, the system should strive to attract and retain teachers and leaders who are committed to and rewarded for excellence. Whereas today's school systems too often favor seniority, obedience, and uniformity, we should work toward a culture of meritocracy and promote organizations in which school leaders have the responsibility, opportunity, and tools for effective leadership. The training pipeline for educators should be rethought to reduce the emphasis on formal certification and focus on selecting quality candidates who add discernible value.

Fourth, education funding should be configured to support new ventures and foster creative problem solving. State and federal regulations require nearly every district to provide similar bundles of services, while districts rarely exploit opportunities to hire specialized providers for human resources, special education, facilities, or remedial instruction. The failure to reward educators who identify cost savings means that there is little impetus to seek cheaper solutions. Education finance should reward cost-effective performance, accommodate nonprofit and for-profit providers of both whole-school and particular services, and ensure that spending is transparent and that malfeasance is promptly addressed.

Finally, a dynamic system demands new knowledge, produced by rigorous models of research and development. This R&D model has already worked well in the medical and technology sectors, where products and services deemed state-of-the-art 20 years ago are now regarded as hopelessly antiquated. There is a need for sustained public investment in basic research; partnerships among practitioners, researchers, and providers who can generate scalable solutions; and an environment that is hospitable to entrepreneurs and established vendors who are willing and able to find ways to leverage new advances so as to serve vast numbers of children, educators, or schools.

Tomorrow's breakthroughs are likely to come from thinkers who are now in junior high schools and playpens and will come of age in the presence of technologies and amidst habits of mind that will always be an acquired taste for those born in 1955 or 1975. Our goal ought not to be the grandiose charge of erecting the "best" educational system with new 21st century buildings and policies that will stand as a monument a half-century from now, but of creating one capable of growing and evolving with those it exists to serve.

Greener Pastures Ahead?

Greenfield accepts the risk that some ventures and ideas will fail in the interest of avoiding a much larger risk: the likelihood that school systems will stagnate amidst old routines, dated rules, and misapplied technology. The entrepreneurial promise does not come with particular brain-based theories of learning or pat guidance on instruction. As such, it can be frustrating for parents and educators because it does not provide a hard-and-fast "solution" to the problems it identifies. Rather, it seeks to nurture excellence by keeping the field open to the skillful application of old models as well as smart efforts to leverage new knowledge, management practices, or technology. Next to such uncertainty, pedigreed programs touted by credentialed experts seem the safer, easier, and more reputable course. Experience, however, suggests that this yearning for surety rarely plays out as hoped.

For all of the excitable headlines and promising successes, the truth is that entrepreneurship is a headache. Entrepreneurship presumes that even smart, thoughtful, well-trained experts cannot anticipate needs, develop solutions, or ensure progress in an orderly fashion. Is it really worth the hassle? The answer is "yes." Every day, our nation's schools fail millions of children and inadequately serve tens of millions more. If forced to compete on performance, many schools and districts might well find themselves out of business, while those schools and districts that excel will find their lives eased or unaffected by greenfield-style reforms. Much of the "hassle" of entrepreneurship, then, is that it makes transparent the mediocrity and failure we otherwise ignore.

In the end, entrepreneurship is not about quick solutions to today's problems. In K–12 schooling, where everyone is quick to state impassioned aims and demand immediate solutions, such a stance is admittedly radical. Nonetheless, the greatest educational risk we confront today lies not in nurturing greenfield but in clinging to the status quo. The uncertainties of greenfield are only worth accepting when compared to the alternative—the stagnation and ceaseless, pointless tinkering that have so long been the face of reform. Ultimately, greenfield reform is a bet on human ingenuity. The secret of successful entrepreneurial sectors is their ability to summon the best within us. Bold, new opportunities have a record of attracting and inspiring talented, motivated individuals in a way that professional hierarchies and public bureaucracies do not. This bet is very different from the one we have historically made in schooling, but, for all that, it may well be the most promising course for 21st century school reform.

NOTES

PREFACE

1. U.S. Department of Education, National Center for Education Statistics, *Schools and Staffing Survey: 2003–04,* http://nces.ed.gov/surveys/sass/index.asp.
2. MetLife, *A MetLife Survey of Teachers, Principals, and Students: Past, Present, and Future,* http://www.metlife.com/assets/cao/contributions/citizenship/teacher-survey-25th-anniv-2008.pdf.
3. Dianna Miller, quoted in Michelle R. Davis, "Advanced Placement Secures Online Niche," *Education Week,* March 26, 2009, 14.

CHAPTER 1

1. Joel Klein, "Leading Change in Public Education" (keynote address to the National Charter Schools Conference, Washington, DC, June 23, 2009), available from http://www.publiccharters.org/KleinKeynoteNCSC09.
2. Joseph A. Schumpeter, *Capitalism, Socialism and Democracy* (New York: Harper, 1975).
3. Clayton M. Christensen and Michael E. Raynor, *The Innovator's Solution: Creating and Sustaining Successful Growth* (Boston: Harvard Business School, 2003), 73.
4. Frederick M. Hess, *Spinning Wheels: The Politics of Urban School Reform* (Washington, DC: Brookings Institution Press, 1999), 95.
5. Richard F. Elmore, *School Reform from the Inside Out: Policy, Practice and Performance* (Cambridge, MA: Harvard Education Press, 2004).
6. Del Stover, "Reform School," *American School Board Journal* 195, no. 11 (2008): 15–18.

7. Frederick M. Hess, "The Bersin Chapter: Nation Can Gain Much Knowledge from San Diego's Experience," *San Diego Union-Tribune*, April 27, 2005, G1.

8. Elissa Gootman and David Herszenhorn, "Getting Smaller to Improve the Big Picture," *New York Times*, May 3, 2005, B2.

9. Larry Cuban, *As Good as It Gets: What School Reform Brought to Austin* (Cambridge, MA: Harvard University Press, 2009).

10. Larry Cuban, *Oversold and Underused: Computers in the Classroom* (Cambridge, MA: Harvard University Press, 2001).

11. Terry M. Moe and John E. Chubb, *Liberating Learning: Technology, Politics, and the Future of American Education* (New York: Jossey-Bass, 2009).

12. Clayton Christensen, Curtis W. Johnson, and Michael B. Horn, *Disrupting Class: How Disruptive Innovation Will Change the Way the World Learns* (New York: McGraw-Hill, 2008).

13. David Tyack and Larry Cuban, *Tinkering Toward Utopia: A Century of Public School Reform* (Cambridge, MA: Harvard University Press, 1995); Hess, *Spinning Wheels*.

14. Robert Stillwell and Lee Hoffman, *Public School Graduates and Dropouts from the Common Core of Data: School Year 2005–06* (report prepared for the U.S. Department of Education, National Center for Education Statistics, January 2009), 5.

15. Christopher B. Swanson, *Cities in Crisis, Special Analytic Report on High School Graduation* (prepared for the Editorial Projects in Education Research Center, April 1, 2008), 1, http://www.americaspromise.org/uploadedFiles/AmericasPromiseAlliance/Dropout_Crisis/SWANSONCitiesInCrisis040108.pdf.

16. Ibid., 9.

17. Frederick M. Hess, *Common Sense School Reform* (New York: Palgrave McMillan, 2004); Abigail M. Thernstrom and Stephan Thernstrom, *No Excuses: Closing the Racial Gap in Learning* (New York: Simon and Schuster, 2003).

18. Paul T. Hill, quoted in Frederick M. Hess and Lance D. Fusarelli, "Cages of Their Own Design?: Superintendents and the Law" (speech prepared for the American Enterprise Institute/Thomas B. Fordham Institute conference "From *Brown* to 'Bong Hits': Assessing a Half-Century of Judicial Involvement in Education," Washington, DC, October 15, 2008).

19. Jean Johnson and Ann Duffet, *I'm Calling My Lawyer: How Litigation, Due Process and Other Regulatory Requirements Are Affecting Public*

Education (pilot study report from Public Agenda and Common Good, January 1, 2003), 9, http://www.publicagenda.org/files/pdf/im_calling_my_lawyer.pdf.

20. Clair Brown, John Haltiwanger, and Julia Lane, *Economic Turbulence: Is a Volatile Economy Good for America?* (Chicago: University of Chicago Press, 2006).

21. *The Economist*, April 18, 1992, quoted in Peter Senge, Art Kleiner, Charlotte Roberts, Rick Ross, George Roth, and Bryan Smith, *Dance of Change: The Challenges of Sustaining Momentum in Learning Organizations* (New York: Doubleday, 1999), 5–6.

22. Paul Strebel, "Why Do Employees Resist Change?" *Harvard Business Review* (May–June 1996): 86.

23. Senge and others, *Dance of Change*, 6.

24. Clayton M. Christensen, *The Innovator's Dilemma: When New Technologies Cause Great Firms to Fail* (Cambridge, MA: Harvard Business School Press, 1997).

25. Michael Kinsley, "Life After Newspapers," *Washington Post*, April 6, 2009, A15.

26. Ibid.

27. Bryan C. Hassel, "Attracting Entrepreneurs to K–12," in *The Future of Educational Entrepreneurship: Possibilities for School Reform*, ed. Frederick M. Hess (Cambridge, MA: Harvard Education Press, 2008), 46–47; Kim Smith and Julie Petersen, "What Is Educational Entrepreneurship?" in Hess, *Educational Entrepreneurship*, 25–26.

28. Wendy Kopp, *One Day All Children . . . : The Unlikely Triumph of Teach For America and What I Learned Along the Way* (New York: Public Affairs, 2001), 19.

29. Bryan Hassel and Julie Kowal, *Stimulating Excellence: Unleashing the Power of Innovation in Education* (report prepared for the American Enterprise Institute, Center for American Progress, the Broad Foundation, New Profit, Inc., Public Impact, and the Annie E. Casey Foundation, Washington, DC: AEI Press, May 2009), 12, http://www.americanprogress.org/issues/2009/05/pdf/education_entrepreneurs.pdf.

30. Smith and Peterson, "What Is Educational Entrepreneurship?" 25–26.

31. Ibid., 25.

32. Jeffrey Henig, *Rethinking School Choice: Limits of the Market Metaphor* (Princeton, NJ: Princeton University Press, 1995).

33. Matt Candler, "Supply-Side Reform on the Ground" (paper presented at American Enterprise Institute Conference, "The Supply Side of School Reform and the Future of Educational Entrepreneurship," Washington, DC, October 25, 2007), 5–6.

34. Paul T. Hill, "Entrepreneurship in K–12 Public Education," in *Social Entrepreneurship*, ed. Marilyn L. Kourilsky and William B. Walstad (Dublin, Ireland: Senate Hall, 2003), 67.

35. J. Gregory Dees and Beth Anderson, "For-Profit Social Ventures," in Kourilsky and Walstad, *Social Entrepreneurship*, 13.

36. John Thornhill, "The View of the Future from Davos," *Financial Times*, January 31, 2006, 13.

37. Carl Schramm, *The Entrepreneurial Imperative: How America's Economic Miracle Will Reshape the World (and Change Your Life)* (New York: Collins, 2006), 11, 49, 78.

38. Robert Fairlie, *Kauffman Index of Entrepreneurial Activity, 1996–2006* (Kansas City, MO: Ewing Marion Kauffman Foundation, 2005), 1; Paul D. Reynolds et al., *The Entrepreneur Next Door: Characteristics of Individuals Starting Companies in America: An Executive Summary of the Panel Study of Entrepreneurial Dynamics* (Kansas City, MO: Ewing Marion Kauffman Foundation, 2002), 14; Michael Selz, "Survey Finds 37% of Households Involved in Small-Business Arena," *Wall Street Journal*, December 13, 1996.

39. Jennifer Cheeseman Day, Alex Janus, and Jessica Davis, *Computer and Internet Use in the United States: 2003* (Special Studies Current Population Report prepared for the U.S. Census Bureau, October 2005), 1, http://www.census.gov/prod/2005pubs/p23-208.pdf.

40. *Education Week*, "Technology Counts: Breaking Away from Tradition," Editorial Projects in Education, March 26, 2009, 32, http://www.edweek.org/media/ew/tc/2009/26stc.pdf.

41. Dan Moren, "Analysis: Inside Apple's iPod sales figures," *Macworld*, January 31, 2008, http://www.macworld.com/article/131874/2008/01/ipodsales.html.

CHAPTER 2

1. Clayton M. Christensen and Michael E. Raynor, *The Innovator's Solution: Creating and Sustaining Successful Growth* (Boston: Harvard Business School, 2003), 221.

2. Chris Whittle, *Crash Course: Imagining a Better Future for Public Education* (New York: Riverhead Books, 2005), 129.

3. Jerome Johnston and Linda Toms Barker, eds., *Assessing the Impact of Technology in Teaching and Learning: A Sourcebook for Evaluators* (Ann Arbor: Institute for Social Research, University of Michigan, 2008).

4. Leslie Ehrlich and Bob Russell, "Employment Security and Job Loss: Lessons from Canada's National Railways, 1956–1995," *Labour/Le Travail*, Spring 2003, http://www.historycooperative.org/journals/llt/51/ehrlich.html.

5. Sasha Cavender, "Legends," Forbes.com, October 5, 1998, http://www.forbes.com/asap/1998/1005/126.html (accessed May 1, 2009).

6. "10 facts About Dr Seuss," *BBC News*, March 2, 2004, http://news.bbc.co.uk/2/hi/entertainment/3523393.stm (accessed May 1, 2009).

7. Mike Mueller, *Mustang 1964 1/2–1973* (Osceola, WI: Motorbooks/MBI Publishing Company, 2000), 30.

8. Robert B. Laughlin, "Reinventing Physics: The Search for the Real Frontier," *Chronicle of Higher Education* 53, no. 26 (February 11, 2005): B6.

9. Matt Candler, "Supply-Side Reform on the Ground," in *The Future of Educational Entrepreneurship: Possibilities for School Reform,* ed. Frederick M. Hess (Cambridge, MA: Harvard Education Press, 2008), 144.

10. David Whitman, *Sweating the Small Stuff: Inner-City Schools and the New Paternalism* (Washington, DC: Thomas B. Fordham Institute, 2008).

11. Whittle, *Crash Course*, 88.

12. Mike Feinberg, remarks at "Race to the Top? The Promise—and Challenges—of Charter School Growth," American Enterprise Institute, April 5, 2009, http://www.aei.org/video/101074.

13. College Summit, *Our Outcomes*, http://www.collegesummit.org/aboutus/results_and_metrics/our outcomes/ (accessed August 10, 2009).

14. Milton Friedman, "Using the Market for Social Development," *Cato Journal* 8, no. 3 (1989): 568.

15. Robert Devlin, Antoni Estevadeordal, and Andrés Rodríguez-Clare, eds. *The Emergence of China: Opportunities and Challenges for Latin America and the Caribbean* (Cambridge, MA: Harvard University Press, 2006).

16. Shahid Javed Burki, "China: The New Global Giant," in *Transforming Socialist Economies: Lessons from Cuba and Beyond*, ed. Shahid Javed Burki and Daniel P. Erikson (New York: Palgrave Macmillan, 2005), 145.

17. Steven A. Morrison and Clifford Winston, "The Remaining Role for Government Policy in the Deregulated Airline Industry," in *Deregulation of Network Industries: What's Next*, ed. Sam Peltzman and Clifford Winston (Washington, DC: AEI-Brookings Joint Center for Regulatory Studies, 2000), 22.

18. William D. Bygrave, "The Entrepreneurial Process," in *The Portable MBA in Entrepreneurship*, 3rd ed., ed. William D. Bygrave and Andrew Zacharakis (Hoboken, NJ: John Wiley and Sons, 2004), 1–27.

19. Thomson Financial Venture Economics/National Venture Capital Association, "Private Equity Enjoyed Record Fundraising Year in 2005" (press release, January 17, 2006), http://www.nvca.org/pdf/FundraisingQ42005final.pdf.

20. Zoltan J. Acs et al., *Global Entrepreneurship Monitor: 2004 Executive Report* (Babson Park, MA: Global Entrepreneurship Monitor, May 2005), tables 1 and 3, http://www.gemconsortium.org/download.asp?fid=364.

21. Anthony S. Bryk and Louis M. Gomez, "Reinventing a Research and Development Capacity," in Hess, *The Future of Educational Entrepreneurship*, 181–82.

22. Hugh Burkhardt and Alan H. Schoenfeld, "Improving Educational Research: Toward a More Useful, More Influential, and Better-Funded Enterprise," *Educational Researcher* 32, no. 9 (December 2003): 3–14.

23. Whittle, *Crash Course*, 30. Whittle estimates an even smaller amount, $260 million per year, is spent currently in the United States on educational R&D.

24. Larry Berger and David Stevenson, "Barriers to Entry: Tales from a Toolbuilder," in Hess, *The Future of Educational Entrepreneurship*, 124.

25. Sara Gambrill, "Venture Philanthropy Is on the Rise, Reaches $75M in 2007," *Clinical Trials Today*, August 13, 2007, http://www.clinicaltrialstoday.com/2007/08/venture-philant.html.

26. Laurence Bloom, "K–13 Education: 2007 Final Market Size and Share Report," *Outsell*, July 23, 2008, http://www.outsellinc.com/store/products/747 (accessed May 1, 2009).

27. J. Gregory Dees and Beth Anderson, "For-Profit Social Ventures," in *Social Entrepreneurship*, ed. Marilyn Kourilsky and William B. Walstad, 1–26 (Dublin, Ireland: Senate Hall, 2003).

CHAPTER 3

1. Alexander Russo, "The Waiting Game," *Education Next* 4, no. 3 (Summer 2004): 48.

2. Terry M. Moe, "The Politics of Bureaucratic Structure," in *Can the Government Govern?* ed. John E. Chubb and Paul E. Peterson (Washington, DC: The Brookings Institution, 1989).

3. Center for Education Reform, *National Charter School Data*, October 2008, http://www.edreform.com/_upload/CER_charter_numbers.pdf.

4. National Governors Association, "High-Quality Charter Schools Create High-Achieving Students" (press release, April 16, 2009), http://www. nga.org/portal/site/nga/menuitem.6c9a8a9ebc6ae07eee28aca9501010a0/ ?vgnextoid=072840abf10b0210VgnVCM1000005e00100aRCRD.

5. Education Commission of the States, *State Notes: Charter School Caps*, http:// mb2.ecs.org/reports/Report.aspx?id=80 (accessed April 21, 2009).

6. Public Impact and WestEd, *Supporting Charter School Excellence Through Quality Authorizing: Innovations in Education* (report prepared for the U.S. Department of Education, Office of Innovation and Improvement, June 2007), 2, http://www.eric.ed.gov/ERICDocs/data/ericdocs2sql/ content_storage_01/0000019b/80/33/c3/be.pdf.

7. Daniel de Vise, "Thriving in District, Charter Schools Are Shunned in Suburbs," *Washington Post*, April 4, 2009, A1.

8. Public Impact and WestEd, *Supporting Charter School Excellence*, 2.

9. Chester Finn and Eric Osberg, *Charter School Funding: Inequity's Next Frontier* (report prepared for the Thomas B. Fordham Institute, Progress Analytics Institute and Public Impact, August 2005), v.

10. Ibid., 1.

11. Shaka L. A. Mitchell and Jeanne Allen, eds., *Solving the Charter School Funding Gap: The Seven Major Causes and What to Do About Them* (Washington, DC: Center for Education Reform, 2005), http://www.edreform. com/_upload/CER-CSFundingGap2005.pdf.

12. Patrick McGuinn, "The Policy Landscape," in *Educational Entrepreneurship: Realities, Challenges, Possibilities*, ed. Frederick M. Hess (Cambridge, MA: Harvard Education Press, 2006), 74.

13. Education Commission of the States, *State Notes: Waivers*, http:// mb2.ecs.org/reports/Report.aspx?id=92 (accessed April 21, 2009).

14. Kara Finnigan et al., *Evaluation of the Public Charter Schools Program: Final Report* (prepared for the U.S. Department of Education, Office of the Deputy Secretary, Policy and Program Studies Service, 2004), 31, http://www.ed.gov/rschstat/eval/choice/pcsp-final/finalreport.pdf.

15. Ibid.

16. C. Emily Feistritzer, *Alternative Teacher Certification: A State-by-State Analysis*, National Center for Education Information, 2007, www. teach-now.org/ATC2007%20Intro.doc (accessed April 21, 2009).

17. Paul T. Decker, Daniel P. Mayer, and Steven Glazerman, *The Effects of Teach For America on Students: Findings from a National Evaluation* (report prepared by Mathematica Policy Research Inc. for the Smith Richardson Foundation, the William and Flora Hewlett Foundation, and the Carnegie Corporation, June 9, 2004), http://www.mathematica-mpr.com/publications/pdfs/teach.pdf.

18. Kate Walsh and Sandi Jacobs, *Alternative Certification Isn't Alternative* (report prepared for the Thomas B. Fordham Institute and the National Council on Teacher Quality, September 2007), 14, http://www.epi.elps.vt.edu/Perspectives/AlternativeCertification07.pdf.

19. National Council on Teacher Quality, *State Teacher Policy Yearbook: Progress on Teacher Quality*, 2007, http://www.nctq.org/stpy/primaryFindings.jsp (accessed April 24, 2009).

20. Walsh and Jacobs, *Alternative Certification Isn't Alternative*, 9.

21. Karla Toye, Rolfe K. Blank, Nancy Sanders, and Andra Williams, *Key State Education Policies on PK–12 Education: 2006* (Washington, DC: Council of Chief State School Officers), 32–33, http://www.ccsso.org/publications/details.cfm?PublicationID=348.

22. Susan M. Gates et al., *Who Is Leading Our Schools? An Overview of School Administrators and their Careers* (Arlington, VA: RAND Education, 2003).

23. As Emily Feistritzer has noted, school administrators are generally viewed and trained as instructional leaders rather than CEOs. C. Emily Feistritzer, *Better Leaders for America's Schools: A Manifesto* (report prepared for the Broad Foundation and the Thomas B. Fordham Institute, May 2003), available from http://www.edexcellence.net/doc/manifesto.pdf.

24. Rick Hess, *Stimulating Excellence: Unleashing the Power of Innovation in Education* (report prepared for the American Enterprise Institute, Center for American Progress, the Broad Foundation, New Profit, Inc., Public Impact, and the Annie E. Casey Foundation, Washington, DC: AEI Press, May 2009) 12, http://www.americanprogress.org/issues/2009/05/pdf/education_entrepreneurs.pdf.

25. Siobhan Gorman, "Selling Supplemental Services," *Education Next* 4, no. 4 (2004): 32.

26. Jeffrey Cohen, testimony provided at the U.S. House Committee on Education and the Workforce Hearing on the Supplemental Education Services (SES) of NCLB, April 26, 2005, http://republicans.edlabor.house.gov/archive/hearings/109th/fc/ses042605/cohen.htm.

27. Douglas Harris, "Class Size and School Size: Taking the Tradeoffs Seriously," in *Brookings Papers on Education Policy*, ed. Frederick M. Hess and Tom Loveless (Washington, DC: Brookings Institution Press, 2006–07), 142–43; Peter Schrag, "Policy from the Hip: Class-Size Reduction in California," in *Brookings Papers on Education Policy*, 238.

28. Steven Wilson, "Opportunities, but a Resistant Culture," in Hess, *Educational Entrepreneurship*, 198.

29. John E. Chubb, "The Bias Against Scale and Profit," in Hess, *Educational Entrepreneurship*, 205.

30. Lowell C. Rose and Alec M. Gallup, "The 38th Annual *Phi Delta Kappa/Gallup Poll* of the Public's Attitudes Toward the Public Schools," *Phi Delta Kappan* 88, no. 1 (2006): 41–56.

31. Terry Moe, *Schools, Vouchers, and the American Public* (Washington, DC: Brookings Institution Press, 2002).

32. Joe Williams, "Games Charter Opponents Play: How Local School Boards—and Their Allies—Block the Competition," *Education Next* 7, no. 1 (2007): 13–18.

33. Ibid., 14.

34. Ibid., 15.

35. Ibid., 18.

36. Ibid.

37. Ed Kirby, "Breaking Regulatory Barriers to Reform," in *The Future of Educational Entrepreneurship: Possibilities for School Reform*, ed. Frederick M. Hess (Cambridge, MA: Harvard Education Press, 2008), 213.

38. Ibid.

39. Larry Berger and David Stevenson, "Barriers to Entry: Tales from a Tool Builder," in Hess, *Educational Entrepreneurship*, 129.

40. Ibid.

41. Ibid.

42. Ibid.

43. Williams, "Games Charter Opponents Play," 16.

44. Henry Levin, "Why Is This So Difficult?" in Hess, *Educational Entrepreneurship*, 173.

45. Ibid.

46. Frederick M. Hess and Coby Loup, *The Leadership Limbo: Teacher Labor Agreements in America's Fifty Largest School Districts* (Washington, DC: Thomas B. Fordham Institute, 2008).

47. Dale Ballou, *Teacher Contracts in Massachusetts* (report prepared for the Pioneer Institute for Public Policy, June 2000, viii, http://www.pioneer institute.org/pdf/wp12.pdf.

48. Mitch Price, *Teacher Union Contracts and High School Reform*, Center on Reinventing Public Education, January 2009, http://www.crpe.org/cs/crpe/download/csr_files/pub_crpe_unioncont_jan09.pdf.

49. Frederick M. Hess and Andrew P. Kelly, "Learning to Lead: What Gets Taught in Principal-Preparation Programs," *Teachers College Record* 109, no. 1 (2007): 244–74.

50. Thomas J. Sergiovanni, *Moral Leadership: Getting to the Heart of School Improvement* (San Francisco: Jossey-Bass, 1996), xiv.

51. Ted Kolderie, "The Other Half of the Strategy: Following Up on System Reform by Innovating with School and Schooling," *Education Evolving*, February 2008, http://www.educationevolving.org/pdf/Innovatingwith schooling.pdf.

CHAPTER 4

1. Chester E. Finn Jr., "Quality Control in a Dynamic Sector," in *The Future of Educational Entrepreneurship: Possibilities for School Reform*, ed. Frederick M. Hess (Cambridge, MA: Harvard Education Press, 2008), 164.

2. Ibid., 171.

3. Richard Rothstein, Rebecca Jacobson, and Tamara Wilder, *Grading Education: Getting Accountability Right* (New York: Economic Policy Institute and Teachers College Press, 2008).

4. Frederick M. Hess and Jon Fullerton, "Balanced Scorecards and Management Data" (working paper prepared for the Center for Education Policy Research at Harvard University, February 2009), http://www.aei.org/paper/100004.

5. Finn, "Quality Control in a Dynamic Sector," 177.

6. Matt Candler, "Supply-Side Reform on the Ground," in Hess, *The Future of Educational Entrepreneurship*, 149–150.

7. Julie Bennett, "Brand-Name Charters," *Education Next* 8, no. 3 (2008): 30.

8. Ibid., 31.

9. Ibid., 32.

CHAPTER 5

1. Glenda Rakes, Brenda Gulledge, and Thomas Rakes, "Quality Assurance in Teacher Education: Warranty Programs," *National Forum of Teacher Education Journal* 16, no. 3 (2005–06): 1.

2. Thomas D. Snyder, Sally A. Dillow, and Charlene M. Hoffman, *Digest of Education Statistics 2008* (report prepared for the U.S. Department of Education, National Center for Education Statistics, March 2009), 53, http://nces.ed.gov/pubs2009/2009020.pdf. Note that if policymakers had maintained the same overall pupil/teacher ratio over that time, we would need 1 million fewer teachers, training could be focused on a smaller and more able population, and average teacher pay would be close to $75,000 per year.

3. Ed Michaels, Helen Handfield-Jones, and Beth Axelrod, *The War for Talent* (Boston: Harvard Business School Press, 2001), xxii.

4. Charles Fishman, "The War for Talent," *Fast Company* 16 (July 1998): 104.

5. Elizabeth Axelrod, Helen Handfield-Jones, and Timothy Walsh, "The War for Talent, Part Two," *McKinsey Quarterly*, May 2001, 1.

6. Vivek Agrawal, James Manyika, and John Richard, "Matching People and Jobs," *McKinsey Quarterly*, June 2003, 5; Allan Schweyer, "An Internal War for Talent," *Inc.*, April 2005, http://www.inc.com/resources/recruiting/articles/20050401/talent wars.html (accessed May 1, 2009).

7. Christopher Gergen and Gregg Vanourek, "Talent Development: Looking Outside the Education Sector," in *The Future of Educational Entrepreneurship: Possibilities for School Reform*, ed. Frederick M. Hess (Cambridge, MA: Harvard Education Press, 2008), 38.

8. Richard Florida, "The Rise of the Creative Class," *Washington Monthly*, May 2002, http://www.washingtonmonthly.com/features/2001/0205.florida.html; Richard Florida, *The Rise of the Creative Class and How It's Transforming Work, Leisure, Community, and Everyday Life* (New York: Perseus Books Group, 2002).

9. U.S. Department of Education, National Center for Education Statistics, *2003–04 Schools and Staffing Survey*, 2007, http://www.nces.ed.gov/pubsearch/getpubcats.asp?sid=003 (accessed May 1, 2009); U. S. Department of Education, National Center for Education Statistics, *1990–91 Schools and Staffing Survey*, 1993, http://www.nces.ed.gov/pubsearch/getpubcats.asp?sid=003# (accessed May 1, 2009).

10. Peter D. Hart Research Associates Inc., *Teaching as a Second Career* (Princeton, NJ: Woodrow Wilson National Fellowship Foundation, September 2008).

11. C. Emily Feistritzer, *Profile of Alternate Route Teachers* (Washington, DC: National Center for Education Information, 2005), 33.

12. Gergen and Vanourek, "Talent Development," 38.

13. Kaya Henderson, "An Army of Great Teachers?" (remarks, American Enterprise Institute, Washington, DC, March 24, 2009).

14. Elinor Mills, "Who's Who of Google Hires," *CNetNews.com*, February 27, 2006, http://news.cnet.com/whos-who-of-Google-hires/2100-1030_3-6043231.html?tag=macol (accessed September 30, 2009).

15. Gary Hamel, "Management à la Google," *Wall Street Journal,* April 26, 2006, A16.

16. Gary Erickson with Lois Lorentzen, *Raising the Bar: Integrity and Passion in Life and Business: The Story of Clif Bar & Co.* (San Francisco: Jossey-Bass, 2004).

17. Wendy Kopp, *One Day, All Children . . . : The Unlikely Triumph of Teach For America and What I Learned Along the Way* (New York: Public Affairs, 2001), 65.

18. James O'Toole and Edward Lawler III, "A Piece of Work," *Fast Company,* 106 (June 2006): 87.

19. Steve Farkas, Jean Johnson, and Ann Duffett, *Stand by Me: What Teachers Really Think About Unions, Merit Pay, and Other Professional Matters* (New York: Public Agenda, 2003), 43, http://www.publicagenda.org/files/pdf/stand_by_me.pdf.

20. Arthur Levine, *Educating School Teachers* (Washington, DC: The Education Schools Project, September 2006), http://www.edschools.org/pdf/Educating_Teachers_Report.pdf.

21. Michaels, Handfield-Jones, and Axelrod, *The War for Talent*, 29, 11.

22. Tamara Erickson and Lynda Gratton, "What It Means to Work Here," *Harvard Business Review,* March 1, 2007, http://hbr.harvardbusiness.org/2007/03/what-it-means-to-work-here/ar/1.

23. Ibid.

24. Gergen and Vanourek, "Talent Development," 32.

25. Hamel, "Management à la Google," A16.

26. John Koten, "A Conversation with Scott Cook," *Inc.*, September 2007, 214.

27. Henderson, "An Army of Great Teachers?"

28. Ryan Hill, statement for the United States Commission on Civil Rights, April 17, 2009.

29. Henderson, "An Army of Great Teachers?"

30. Jay P. Greene, "Steven Jobs Has Guts," *New York Sun*, February 21, 2007, http://www.nysun.com/opinion/steve-jobs-has-guts/48971/.

31. Steve Farkas, Jean Johnson, and Ann Duffett, *Rolling Up Their Sleeves: Superintendents and Principals Talk About What's Needed to Fix Public Schools* (New York: Public Agenda, 2003), 39.

32. Arthur Levine, *Educating School Leaders* (report prepared for the Education Schools Project, March 2005), http://www.edschools.org/reports_leaders.htm.

33. Teach For America, *Admissions*, http://www.teachforamerica.org/admissions/index.htm (accessed May 1, 2009).

34. Teach For America, *Connecticut*, http://www.teachforamerica.org/about/regions/connecticut.htm (accessed May 1, 2009).

35. Bridget Kelly, *Connecting the Dots: Staying Power: Teach For America Alumni in Public Education* (Washington, DC: Education Sector, 2006), http://www.educationsector.org/usr_doc/TFA_Dots.pdf. (accessed May 1, 2009).

36. Teach For America, *Alumni Effecting Fundamental Change*, http://www.teachforamerica.org/mission/our_impact/alumni_fundamental_change.htm (accessed April 21, 2009).

37. Education Pioneers, *Strategy & Impact*, http://www.educationpioneers.org/what-we-do/strategy-impact (accessed May 1, 2009).

38. Monica C. Higgins, *Career Imprints: Creating Leaders Across an Industry* (San Francisco: Jossey-Bass, 2005); Monica C. Higgins and Frederick M. Hess, "The Challenges for Charter Schools," *Education Outlook Series* (Washington, DC: American Enterprise Institute, April 2009), http://www.aei.org/outlook/100025.

39. Matt Candler, "Supply-Side Reform on the Ground," in Hess, *The Future of Educational Entrepreneurship*, 155.

40. Ibid., 160.

41. Julie Bennett, "Brand-Name Charters," *Education Next* 8, no. 3 (2008): 31.

CHAPTER 6

1. Jay Mathews, *Work Hard, Be Nice: How Two Inspired Teachers Created America's Best Schools* (Chapel Hill, N.C.: Algonquin Books, 2009), 91.

2. Wendy Kopp, *One Day All Children . . . : The Unlikely Triumph of Teach For America and What I Learned Along the Way* (New York: Public Affairs, 2001), 11.

3. Ibid., 46.

4. PricewaterhouseCoopers/National Venture Capital Association, *Money Tree Report: Investments by Region Q1 1995–Q4 2008*, January 24, 2009, http://www.nvca.org/index.php?option=com_content&view=article&id=78:latest-industry-statistics&catid=40:research&Itemid=102.

5. National Venture Capital Association, *Venture Impact: The Economic Importance of Venture Capital Backed Companies to the U.S. Economy*, 4th ed. (Arlington, VA: National Venture Capital Association, 2007).

6. PricewaterhouseCoopers/National Venture Capital Association, *Money Tree Report*.

7. Joe Keeney and Daniel Pianko, "Catalyzing Capital Investment: Lessons from Outside Education," in *The Future of Educational Entrepreneurship: Possibilities for School Reform*, ed. Frederick M. Hess (Cambridge, MA: Harvard Education Press, 2008), 69.

8. Eric Bassett, Catherine Burdt, and J. Mark Jackson, *The Education Investor: 2004 Year-End Review and Outlook* (Boston: Eduventures, 2005).

9. Scott Shane, *Fool's Gold: The Truth About Angel Investing in America* (New York: Cambridge University Press USA, 2008).

10. *The PRI Directory* (New York: The Foundation Center, 2003).

11. Chuck Harris, interview in *Philanthropy News Daily* (September 28, 2007), 1, http://www.seachangecap.org/news/seachange-pnd-092807.pdf.

12. Ibid., 2.

13. Wendy Hassett and Dan Katzir, "Lessons Learned from the Inside," in *With the Best of Intentions*, ed. Frederick M. Hess (Cambridge, MA: Harvard Education Press, 2005), 239.

14. Marguerite Roza and Karen Hawley Miles, *A New Look at Inequities in School Funding: A Presentation on the Resource Variations Within Districts* (Seattle: Center on Reinventing Public Education, May 2002), 9.

15. Paul T. Hill, "Entrepreneurship in K–12 Public Education," in *Social Entrepreneurship*, ed. Marilyn L. Kourilsky and William B. Walstad (Dublin, Ireland: Senate Hall, 2003), 71.

16. U.S. Department of Education, Office of Communications and Outreach, *Guide to U.S. Department of Education Programs* (Washington, DC, 2008), 228, http://www.ed.gov/programs/gtep/gtep.pdf.

17. U.S. Department of Education, *State Charter School Facilities Incentive Grants*, http://www.ed.gov/programs/statecharter/gtepstatecharter.pdf (accessed May 1, 2009).

18. Frederick M. Hess, *Stimulating Excellence: Unleashing the Power of Innovation in Education* (report prepared for the American Enterprise Institute, Center for American Progress, the Broad Foundation, New Profit, Inc., Public Impact, and the Annie E. Casey Foundation, Washington, DC: AEI Press, May 2009), 31, http://www.americanprogress.org/issues/2009/05/pdf/education_entrepreneurs.pdf.

19. Vermont Sustainable Jobs Fund, *Our Approach*, http://www.vsjf.org/about/our_approach.shtml (accessed April 7, 2009); Adele Holoch, "The Means to Be Daring and Innovative," *Burlington Free Press*, April 10, 2006, http://highmowingseeds.com/pdfs/BFP_VSJF_4-10-06.pdf; Tim Traver, "New Approach to Economic Development in Vermont," *Business* 26, no. 2 (2004), http://www.jgpress.com/inbusiness/archives/_free/000612.html.

20. Jay P. Greene, "Buckets into the Sea: Why Philanthropy Isn't Changing Schools, and How It Could," in Hess, *With the Best of Intentions*.

21. Hassett and Katzir, "Lessons Learned from the Inside," 240.

22. "How Venture Philanthropy Is Working to Change Education" (*Education Week* online conversation with Janet Knupp and Judith Feldman, moderated by Dakarai I. Aarons, January 30, 2009), http://www.edweek.org/chat/transcript_01_30_09.html?r=2112600612 (accessed March 6, 2009).

23. Tom Vander Ark, "Private Capital and Public Education: Toward Quality at Scale" (Future of American Education Working Paper, American Enterprise Institute, 2009), 13.

24. Ted Mitchell, quoted in Hess, *Stimulating Excellence*, 32.

25. Andrew Wolk, *Advancing Social Entrepreneurship: Recommendations for Policy Makers and Government Agencies* (report prepared for the Aspen Institute/Root Cause, April 2008), http://www.aspeninstitute.org/sites/default/files/content/docs/join%20our%20mailing%20lists/nspp_AdvSocEntrp.pdf; for background information, see *Mobilizing Change: 10 Non-profit Policy Proposals to Strengthen U.S. Communities*, The Aspen Institute, 2008, http://www.aspeninstitute.org/sites/default/files/content/docs/pubs/mobilizing_change.pdf.

26. Keeney and Pianko, "Catalyzing Capital Investment," 65–88.

CHAPTER 7

1. Matt Candler, "The Supply Side of School Reform and the Future of Educational Entrepreneurship" (remarks, American Enterprise Institute, Washington, DC, October 25, 2007).

2. Paul Tough, *Whatever It Takes: Geoffrey Canada's Quest to Change Harlem and America* (Boston: Houghton Mifflin, 2008), 19.

3. Mike Feinberg, remarks at "Race to the Top? The Promise—and Challenges—of Charter School Growth," American Enterprise Institute, April 5, 2009, http://www.aei.org/video/101074.

4. William A. Sahlman, "How to Write a Great Business Plan," *Harvard Business Review*, July–August 1997, http://hbr.harvardbusiness.org/1997/07/how-to-write-a-great-business-plan/ar/1.

5. Jim Collins, *Good to Great: Why Some Companies Make the Leap . . . and Others Don't* (New York: HarperBusiness, 2001), 20, 39.

6. Kim Smith and Julie Peterson, "Social Purpose Capital Markets," in *The Future of Educational Entrepreneurship: Possibilities for School Reform*, ed. Frederick M. Hess (Cambridge, MA: Harvard Education Press, 2008).

7. Das Narayandas, "Building Loyalty in Business Markets," *Harvard Business Review*, September 2005, http://hbr.harvardbusiness.org/2000/50/building-loyalty-in-business-markets/ar/1.

8. Larry Berger and David Stevenson, "Barriers to Entry: Tales from a Tool Builder," in Hess, *The Future of Educational Entrepreneurship*, 130.

9. InsideSchools.org, "Review: The Equity Project Charter School," http://insideschools.org/index12.php?fs=1943&all=y (accessed April 24, 2009).

10. Joe Williams, "Teacher Seniority Rules Nixed for Summer Hires," *New York Daily News*, June 17, 2005, http://www.nydailynews.com/archives/news/2005/06/17/2005-06-17_teacher_seniority_rules_nixe.html.

11. Joel Klein, "Leading Change in Public Education" (keynote address to the National Charter Schools Conference, Washington, DC, June 23, 2009), http://www.publiccharters.org/KleinKeynoteNCS09.

12. Chris Whittle, *Crash Course: Imagining a Better Future for Public Education* (New York: Riverhead Books, 2005), 157–178.

13. Ed Kirby, "Breaking Regulatory Barriers to Reform," in *The Future of Educational Entrepreneurship*, 216.

14. Clayton Christensen, Curtis W. Johnson, and Michael B. Horn, *Disrupting Class: How Disruptive Innovation Will Change the Way the World Learns* (New York: McGraw-Hill, 2008).

15. Clayton Christensen, *The Innovator's Dilemma: When New Technologies Cause Great Firms to Fail* (Cambridge, MA: Harvard Business School Press, 1997).

16. John E. Chubb and Terry M. Moe, *Politics, Markets, and America's Schools* (Washington, DC: Brookings Institution, 1990), 217.

17. Robin Pasquarella, as quoted in "Big Bucks Going Back to School," *Seattle Times*, December 10, 2000, http://community.seattletimes.nwsource.com/archive/?date=20011210&slug=TT8E2J3LO.

18. Bill Gates, speech to the National Governors Association and Achieve, Inc.'s National Education Summit on High Schools, February 26, 2005, http://www.gatesfoundation.org/speeches-commentary/Pages/bill-gates-2005-national-education-summit.aspx.

19. U.S. Chamber of Commerce, *Leaders and Laggards: A State-by-State Report Card on Educational Effectiveness*, February 2007, 82, http://www.uschamber.com/NR/rdonlyres/e6vj565iidmycznvk4ikm3mryxo5nslm7iq2uyrta5vrqdxsagjvkxafz6r3buzaopo4uxv4o4ep4nvhmc3ppc7drjd/USChamberLeadersandLaggards.pdf.

20. David B. Tyack, *The One Best System: A History of American Urban Education* (Cambridge, MA: Harvard University, 1974).

INDEX

The letter *f* following a page number denotes a figure.

ABOUT THE AUTHOR

 **FREDERICK M. HESS** is director of education policy studies at the American Enterprise Institute. A nationally recognized author and commentator on schooling, his books include *Educational Entrepreneurship* (Harvard Education Press, 2006), *Common Sense School Reform* (Palgrave Macmillan, 2004), and *Spinning Wheels* (Brookings Institution, 1998). You will find his research and writings in scholarly and popular periodicals, including *Harvard Educational Review, Teachers College Record, Social Science Quarterly, Educational Leadership, Phi Delta Kappan, Education Week, Washington Post,* and *U.S. News and World Report.* He sits on the boards of directors of StandardsWork and the National Association of Charter School Authorizers, is executive editor of *Education Next,* and is a member of the review board for the Broad Prize in Urban Education.

A former high school social studies teacher, Hess holds an MEd in Teaching and Curriculum and an MA and PhD in Government from Harvard University. He has taught education and public policy at Harvard, Georgetown, and Rice Universities and at the Universities of Pennsylvania and Virginia.

Related ASCD Resources: School Reform

At the time of publication, the following ASCD resources were available (ASCD stock numbers appear in parentheses). For up-to-date information about ASCD resources, go to www.ascd.org.

Books

The Best Schools: How Human Development Research Should Inform Educational Practice by Thomas Armstrong (#106044)

The Big Picture: Education Is Everyone's Business by Dennis Littky with Samantha Grabelle (#104438)

Catching Up or Leading the Way: American Education in the Age of Globalization by Young Zhao (#109076)

Detracking for Excellence and Equity by Carol Corbett Burris and Delia T. Garrity (#108013)

Leading Change in Your School: How to Conquer Myths, Build Commitment, and Get Results by Douglas B. Reeves (#109019)

Results Now: How We Can Achieve Unprecedented Improvements in Teaching and Learning by Mike Schmoker (#106045)

Networks

Visit the ASCD Web site (www.ascd.org) and click on About ASCD. Click on Networks, then Network Directory, for information about professional educators who have formed groups around topics, including "Quality Education," and "Restructuring School."

THE WHOLE CHILD The Whole Child Initiative helps schools and communities create learning environments that allow students to be healthy, safe, engaged, supported, and challenged. To learn more about books and resources that relate to the whole child, visit www.wholechildeducation.org.

For more information, visit us on the World Wide Web (http://www.ascd.org); send an e-mail message to member@ascd.org; call the ASCD Service Center (1-800-933-ASCD or 703-578-9600, then press 2); send a fax to 703-575-5400; or write to Information Services, ASCD, 1703 N. Beauregard St., Alexandria, VA 22311-1714 USA.